SEEKER

TRAVELING THE PATH TO ENLIGHTENMENT

Introduction by Jean Houston

JEREMY P. TARCHER/PUTNAM
A MEMBER OF PENGUIN PUTNAM INC.
NEW YORK

A BOOK LABORATORY BOOK

Most Tarcher/Putnam books are available at special quantity discounts for bulk purchase for sales promotions, premiums, fund-raising, and educational needs. Special books or book excerpts also can be created to fit specific needs. For details, write Putnam Special Markets, 375 Hudson Street, New York, NY 10014.

Jeremy P. Tarcher/Putnam
A member of
Penguin Putnam Inc.
375 Hudson Street
New York, NY 10014
www.penguinputnam.com
Introduction © by Jean Houston
A Nation of Seekers © by Mark Robert Waldman
Designed by Kristen Garneau, Sausalito, CA

Library of Congress Cataloging-in-Publication Data

Seeker: traveling the path to enlightenment / introduction by Jean Houston.
      p. cm.—(Archetypes of the collective unconscious ; vol. 3)
    "A Book Laboratory book"—T.p. verso
  ISBN 1-58542-189-8
    1. American literature. 2. Archetype (Psychology)—Literary collections.
    3. Self-actualization (Psychology)—Literary collections. I. Series.
  PS509.A73S44 2002   2002028702
810.8'0353—dc21

Printed in Singapore
10 9 8 7 6 5 4 3 2 1

TABLE OF CONTENTS

ABOUT THIS SERIES

OUR WORLD IS FILLED WITH ARCHETYPAL IMAGERY, POWERFUL SYMBOLS THAT REFLECT THE DEEPEST LAYERS OF OUR personality—our strengths, weaknesses, and unacknowledged gifts that lay hidden within our souls. Primarily unconscious, these inner forces shape our behaviors, attitudes and beliefs. By exploring these secret desires—in ourselves, through literature and art—we can gain mastery over them, bringing greater consciousness into our lives.

Archetypal themes are universal, for they can be found in every culture throughout history. But each society reflects them in distinctive ways. The American lover, for example, is far more romantic, erotic, and idealized than the images portrayed in Asia. By contrast, the shadow, which is aptly acknowledged in the European psyche, is relatively ignored by Americans. Unlike other cultures, we do not like to peer directly at the darkness that lies within. Instead we project our shadows onto fiction, the movies, or the criminal elements in the world. Even the shadow artists in America are often met with hostility or disdain, especially when the subject offends our moral and religious values. The shadow artist is readily condemned, an unpatriotic pariah that spoils our fantasies and dreams.

The American seeker is also unique amongst the cultures of the world: in our separation of church from state, religion becomes a quest for personal spirituality, one that liberally borrows from other traditions and groups. Our economic and scientific advancements have also transformed the healer archetype from a country shaman into a medical sage.

Artists, poets, and writers help to bring these archetypal forms to life by embracing them in their work. Stephen King, for example, is a master of the shadow, as was Sexton, Poe, and Melville. The spiritual quest of the seeker is vividly captured in the poetry of Whitman and Frost, in the prose of Alice Walker, and in the speeches of Martin Luther King. Even the face of Andrew Weil, alternative medicine's champion, has become a core archetypal symbol of the American healer: wise, warm, and passionately devoted to the integration of body, mind, and soul. And who would not be moved by O'Henry's short story *The Gift of the Magi* in which two lovers sacrifice their most valued possessions to soothe each other's soul?

Art in particular makes a strong impression upon our soul, and in choosing the illustrations to accompany these stories, we have selected unique images that span the breadth and depth of contemporary American painting and photography. From the sun-dappled colors of the impressionists, to the austere contrasts of black and white photography, and from the immediacy of the advertising medium and the obliqueness of the symbolic form, these images hint at the acuity of our inner landscapes and dreams. Mysterious, moody, and serene, they work upon our psyches inviting us to rest the eye upon the symbolic eloquence of life.

May these stories and images guide you inwards as you will witness that wondrous place where a greater consciousness resides.

The wonder of the collective unconscious is that it is all there, all the legend and history of the human race, with its unexorcised demons and its gentle saints, its mysteries and its wisdom, all with each one of us—a microcosm with the macrocosm. The exploration of this world is more challenging than the exploration of the solar system; and the journey to inner space is not necessarily an easy or a safe trip.

—June Singer

The archetype represents a profound riddle surpassing our rational comprehension [expressing] itself first and foremost in metaphors. There is some part of its meaning that always remains unknown and defies formulation.

—Jacobi Jolande

Our personal psychology is just a thin skin, a ripple on the ocean of collective psychology [and] the archetypes are the great decisive forces, they bring about the real events, and not our personal reasoning and practical intellect... .The archetypal images decide the fate of man.

—Carl G. Jung

Series Editor: Mark Robert Waldman
Series conceived by Jeremy P. Tarcher
Series created by Philip Dunn, Manuela Dunn and Book Laboratory
Picture research by Julie Foakes
Design by Kristen Garneau

Other Titles in the Series:
Shadow: Touching the Darkness Within, Volume 1, with an Introduction by Robert Bly
Healer: Transforming Our Inner and Outer Wounds, Volume 2, with an Introduction by Andrew Weil
Lover: Embracing Our Passionate Hearts, Volume 4, with an Introduction by Robert A. Johnson

INTRODUCTION BY JEAN HOUSTON

THERE SHE STANDS AT THE ENTRANCE TO NEW YORK HARBOR, THE GREAT LADY HERSELF, HOLDING THE TORCH OF Liberty, beckoning the seeker to come and find whatever he is searching for. She has become the iconic archetype for those who seek another possibility, the beautiful strange attractor, the lure of becoming to the millions upon millions who have passed her, while en route to new lives in a new land. The lines of Emma Lazarus carved at her base give her passionate words:

> Keep, ancient lands, your storied pomp!" cries she,
> With silent lips, "Give me your tired, your poor,
> Your huddled masses yearning to breathe free,
> The wretched refuse of your teeming shore;
> Send these, the homeless, tempest-tost to me,
> I lift my lamp beside the golden door!

Ninety years ago, my Grandfather, Prospero Todaro, having read some words of Thomas Jefferson, and having seen in the paper a picture of the Statue of Liberty, felt the call of that golden door, and so he gathered up his family, left Sicily and sailed for America. My mother told me that standing on the deck, as soon as he saw the Lady, this usually taciturn man laughed hugely, clapped wildly and shouted, "Brava, brava!"

What is it about America that calls the seeker to trek and meander, sail, wander, and traverse endlessly, searching for a thousand different kinds of riches? For that matter, what is it that drives all of us to seek new realms—physical, mental, emotional, and spiritual? To answer in Native American words, we seek the heart of the Great Mystery by learning to experience the truth of our personal Medicine, as well as our community and global Medicine.

Part of the mystery of America is its place in the global mindfield as the seeker's paradise, the visionary land of freedom and opportunity where there could be realized humankind's millennia-old dreams of the golden age returned to a new land beyond the western waters. This is a critical point and one that we often forget—that America was built on the expectations not just of several hundred years of frustrated Europeans, but on the radical eschatological hopes of millions of people over thousands of years. The hopes of history and the spiritual imagination of many peoples and cultures came to fruition in the very founding of America. From the point of view of the psychodynamics of the planet itself, this is a very potent fact of our existence as a nation, and perhaps explains the relative good fortune we enjoy in the canon of nations. The ground is still charged with the power, pulse, and psyche that brought so many seekers to these shores to be re-charged, reawakened.

Here the chance to reinvent the world was unparalleled, and America spoke to man's natural inventiveness, his innate creativity. And yet the shadows were immense: the million of Africans arriving in hellish vessels to be slaves, the slaughter of the native peoples and the brutal rejection of their spirit, wisdom and integrity. Then there is the fact of the initial settling of America by puritanical sectarian groups whose religion gave them an image of themselves as born-guilty creatures who dared not probe their inner states lest they discover their depraved nature. This lent impetus to work as one sought salvation by justifying one's life through unstinting labor and economic advancement. These things, along with the outward looking of the prevalent frontier psychology, made materialism king, and inhibited the tapping of the deeper strata of the nation's psyche, and the uncovering of the possibilities that were there for art, religion, myth, culture, and consciousness. One has only to look at the work of early and mid-20th century writers like Sinclair Lewis, F. Scott Fitzgerald, Eugene O'Neill, Theodore Dreiser, Lillian Hellman and Edna Ferber to experience the frustration of those who seek "roads of soul" that swing off and away from the Main Streets of Mammon. They tell us in their various ways that Babbit and his buddies betray the essence of America, placing the soul of culture as a satellite to economics rather than economics being a satellite to the soul of culture.

...a sense of completeness is achieved through a union of the consciousness with the unconscious contents of the mind. Out of this union arises what Jung called "the transcendent function of the psyche," by which a man can achieve his highest goal: the full realization of the potential of his individual Self.

—Joseph L. Henderson

But soul will out, and in the American stage and musical we find another street, Broadway, the Great White Way, the American road to its own particular Elusianian mysteries. Here was theater which, like the ancient mysteries, shakes us up vigorously and triumphantly, then realigns us into resonance with the numinous powers, and with the rhythms of the earth, the moon, the sun with love and loss, death and renewal. The Mysteries allow us to sense and strengthen the sense of the eternal within us, and to bask in that vivid, all-encompassing blessing.

When I was a small child, my father, who sometimes worked as a show doctor, took me to the Broadway opening of Rogers and Hammerstein's *Oklahoma,* and several years later to *Carousel.* Here were musicals that carried the dream of the American seeker. *Oklahoma* had everything, including our shadows: the Oklahoma Territory, the cowboys and farmers, statehood and poor Jud Frye, the lonely carrier of the dark side. But through it all, the threnody, "The sound of the earth is like music." *Carousel* makes that loner into the anti-hero, but one whom love redeems and who is able to love from beyond death. One of the great lessons of the mystery plays is that love can and does endure in the Underworld, and one never stops seeking the beloved.

Of all the great musicals, Gershwin's *Porgy and Bess* gave us the most complete experience of mystery, transcendence, and the calling in of the magic of ordinary reality, telling it like it is, even if you've got plenty of nothing, but your Mama's good looking, the Bible ain't necessarily so, and somehow we'll all pull through as we seek the Summertime of a new reality.

But it was the movies that provided the American Seeker with his cult and much of his culture. Here was the oozing of our dreams onto celluloid—soul stuff in high projection. Gone was the hearth where the grandparents told the old tales. We thought we had found something better; we thought we could fall through the screen into mythic lives.

In the trance domain of the darkened theater, we became liminal, incarnating as a shy cowboy single-handedly taking on a gang of cattle rustlers. Losing our boundaries, we became Mr. Smith, an ardent but ordinary Joe, and cleaned up political corruption in Washington. When we plunged into despair, a wingless angel fell out of the sky and helped us revalue our wonderful life.

One movie in particular, *The Wizard of Oz,* gave all seekers a new horizon of life beyond Kansas, beyond outmoded conditions, and entry into the larger domains that are lying just beyond ordinary experience, somewhere over the rainbow. It gave us a sense of our capacity to survive, to surmount evil, to trust in our enormous untapped potentials, and to green the old wasteland. And to do this by taking the hero and heroine's journey into myth, there to discover allies, friends of the soul, companions of the road, and the enormous multidimensional universe that lies nested within reality as well as within each of us. Like all great myths, the story poses the ultimate questions or origins: Where have we come from? Where are we going? Where do we belong? What is the nature of reality and how do we live simultaneously in its various worlds? All of these questions are supported on marvelous waves of mythic imagery with superhuman beings and supernatural forces irrupting into the world of ordinary life. The yellow brick road becomes the golden spirit road of the true seeker, the pilgrim of the soul.

In recent years the American Seeker has been discovering what Dorothy found when she returned to Kansas: that everything she could ever want or know is to be found in her own backyard, that is the backyard of the mind which includes the vaster domains of the subconscious as well as the collective unconscious of the human race and the planetary mind as well. Perhaps that is why the Zeit is getting Geisty and Spirit is emerging everywhere and in combinations as unusual as they are evocative.

Most of the people I meet these days seem to be on a spiritual quest, or if not, they have a growing hunger for it. The hound of heaven woofs at their heels urging them to wake up to their spiritual possibilities and seek their spiritual practice. For sheer creativity and inventiveness, nothing beats spiritual adventuring. People try out religions as different as possible from the ones in which they were raised, go on spiritual shopping sprees, feast at the Divine Deli. As well they may, for the complexity of the present time seems to demand a deepening of our nature if we are going to survive. Deepening requires exploration. And for all its byways, exploration leads ultimately to the spiritual source of our existence.

Not since the days of Plato and Buddha and Confucius, some twenty-five hundred years ago, has there been such an uprising of spiritual yearning. But instead of being a Mediterranean and Asian phenomenon, as it was then, the explosion of spirituality is now happening worldwide. In America alone, in the last twenty years, the number of religious groups has doubled. We take new names, sit zazen, become Sufis, Taoists, neo-pagans, devotees of Kali and Vedanta. Buddhism in all its varieties is the fastest growing American faith.

The world mind, it seems, is forging a new container for its spiritual seekers. Whether it is a new religion or the blending of the best of the old ones—whether it is more universal forms of collective worship or a general intensification of private spiritual practice, something unprecedented is brewing in the Earth's spiritual continuum: a grand company of mystic-minded adventurers, bent on exploring every room in the many-mansioned House of the Holy.

Today, one of the most potent of spiritual phenomena is the rise of the feminine archetype, a time when so many women—and even a few men—are seeking the feminine face of God. I recall my own attempts, at age six, to find the Virgin Mary. I wanted her to appear up front and personal. My father gave me all kinds of satiric questions to ask the poor little nun at school, like "When Jesus rose, was that because God filled him full of helium?" One day, I asked her whether Jesus ever had to go to the bathroom. She finally exploded, giving me hundreds of thousand's of years in Purgatory for each of my theological queries. I ended up with 300 million years in Purgatory, and I went home crying to my father who promptly took me off to see the movie, *The Song of Bernadette.* When we returned home, I sought the Virgin Mary while kneeling in a closet, promising her many sacrifices of candy and cookies if she would only show up like she did for Bernadette. When she did not appear, I gave up and sat by the window, utterly spent, looking out at the fig tree blooming in the back yard. Drowsy and unfocused, I must have unwittingly tapped into the appropriate spiritual doorway, for suddenly the key turned, and the door to the universe opened. Nothing changed in my outward perceptions. There were no visions, no sprays of golden light, certainly no appearance by the Virgin Mary. The world remained as it had been. Yet, everything around me, including myself, moved into meaning. Everything—the fig tree blooming in the yard, the plane in the sky, the sky itself, and even my idea of the Virgin Mary—became part of a single Unity, a glorious symphonic resonance in which every part of the universe was a part of and illuminated every other part, and I knew that in some way, it all worked together, and it was very good. I was in a universe of friendship and fellow feeling, a companionable universe filled with interwoven Presence and the Dance of Life. The sensation lasted about two seconds, but it seemed to go on forever.

Somewhere downstairs, I heard the door slam, and my father,

Self-revelation is a cruel process. The real picture, the real "you" never emerges. Looking for it is as bewildering as trying to know how you really look. Ten different mirrors show you ten different faces.

—Shashi Deshpande

laughing, entered the house. Instantly, the whole universe joined in. Great roars of hilarity sounded from sun to sun. Field mice tittered, and so did angels and rainbows. Laughter leavened every atom and every star until I saw a universe inspirited and spiraled by joy, not unlike the one I later read in Dante's great vision of Paradise. This was a knowledge of the way everything worked—through love and joy and the utter interpenetration of everything with the All That Is.

Experiences such as this are not uncommon, especially for children, nor are they something to be kept sacrosanct in esoteric cupboards. They are coded into our bodies, brimming in our minds, and knocking on the doors of our souls. As a child it charged me and changed me and gave me the impetus to do the things I later did. It showed me the many faces of God, and made me a seeker after spirit, a pilgrim of the possible.

Here, in this collection, are stories and essays that illumine this quest, vibrant tellings of the search for the fundamental reality of THAT which we are ever seeking—only to find that IT is always seeking us.

A NATION OF SEEKERS

Mark Robert Waldman

> *Not since the days of Plato and Buddha and Confucius, some twenty-five hundred years ago, has there been such an uprising of spiritual yearning . . . . The spiritual technologies at our disposal can be harvested from the whole world: Christian centering prayer, Buddhist mindfulness and visualization practices, African trance dancing, Tantra and sacred sexuality, Native American powwows and sweat lodges, shamanic spirit journeys, Asian martial arts, Jungian dreamwork, as well as, for some, the neomystical study of quantum realities. All of these rework the landscapes of the subliminal mind so that there are channels and riverbed in which a deeper spiritual consciousness can flow.*
>
> —Jean Houston, from *Jump Time*

AS A UNIVERSAL ARCHETYPE, THE SEEKER SYMBOLIZES OUR INNER SEARCH FOR WHOLENESS, COMPLETION, EVEN enlightenment—a transcendence of the individual self. On a personal level, the seeker may manifest itself in our search for happiness, love, or wealth. Even the explorer, the adventurer, and the entrepreneur are seekers of something new: an object to uncover, a place to map, a mystery to ponder and resolve. These quests, Jung suggests, are part of an inner spiritual core. Governed by the unconscious processes of the soul, they help to soothe our insecurities and pain.

For most of history, the archetypal seeker was a rare phenomenon, epitomized by an individual who felt spiritually torn or empty. Such a person seeks wisdom or truth, turning inward or upward for a message, a sign, a direction in which to turn. Mohammad was a seeker, as was the Buddha, but the notion of a "nation of seekers" would be born in the United States, due largely to Jefferson's constitutional decree separating church and state:

No man shall be compelled to frequent or support any religious worship,
place, or ministry whatsoever, nor shall [he] … otherwise suffer on
account of his religious opinions or belief; but that all men shall be free
to profess, and by argument to maintain, their opinion in matters of
religion, [and] that the same shall in no wise diminish, enlarge, or affect
their civil capacities.

This principle encouraged Americans to seek spiritual satisfaction in whatever manner they chose, leading eventually to the establishment, as the *Encyclopedia of Religions in the United States* illuminates, of over one thousand religious sects. For nearly two centuries, our country has been a refuge for spiritual diversity, for where else can one witness Catholics, Muslims, Buddhists, Hindus, and Jews coexisting with atheists, agnostics, and a hodgepodge of New Age ideals? Truly, we are a nation of seekers, fighting for equality in a world still stricken by religious discord.

Our most recent revolution of spirit took place in the 1960s, when thousands of young Americans questioned traditional morals and searched for alternative values and faith. For many, the social principles of Martin Luther King took hold, while others sought anchorage in spiritual beliefs from abroad. Colleges imported gurus and scientists studied shamanic herbs. Experiments proliferated, yet a common thread remained: American seekers sought enlightenment from within, borrowing heavily from the psychological models of that day. This newfound spirituality had profound effects upon society, bringing radical changes to organized religion and education. In the field of medicine, new healing modalities emerged. For example, our current stress reduction techniques are based on the principles of meditation and prayer.

In the stories, memoirs, and art that appear in this book, the many faces of the seeker unfold, illuminating our journeys into the sacredness of life. We find the seeker in Robert Frost's poem, *The Road Not Taken*, and in the opening passages of *Siddhartha,* a tale by Herman Hesse that inspired many young Americans to rethink their notions of truth. An essay by the Dalai Lama is also included because he has deeply influenced our spiritual perspectives and dreams.

Our children's books, and the films they have generated, also reflect the archetypal spirit of the seeker, as we see in *The Wizard of Oz,* Frank Baum's enduring story of a girl in search of enlightenment and love. But it is Dorothy's faith, embedded in her goodness and innocence, that eventually brings her home. The message for all seekers is the same: no matter how far we travel, no matter what adventures ensue, we must always, *always,* come home.

Other tales reveal unusual predicaments that seekers often stumble upon, as the heroine in Daniel Barthelme's short story discovers. She finds herself in a city of churches where everyone must participate, but she refuses to cooperate. The question is raised: do we each have the courage to maintain our personal vision and faith, even when those around us object? In other memoirs, the seeker finds refuge in nature, in the mystery of life and death, even in the backseat of a cab, as Foster Furcolo's protagonist does. Be it in the struggle of Doris Colmes' homeless young man, or the salvation proffered in a Twelve-Step recovery pledge, we feel these archetypal forces at work, bringing us consciousness, compassion, even joy.

But the search for enlightenment is not easy, for with each new insight old beliefs must change. If this does not occur, then the shadow side of the seeker erupts, generating prejudice and fear towards those of differing ideals. "Sinners in the Hands of an Angry God," the infamous sermon penned in 1741, captures a darkness that continues to haunt our world.

In a nation such as ours, we cannot avoid being seekers, but how do we manifest our search when the path requires years of reflection and work? And how do we bring our spirituality into the world without impinging on the values of others? If our seeking brings a sense of well being, how might we bring these benefits to bear upon our inner-city conflicts, and to others who suffer in this world? Through volunteering? Through charitable contributions? Even, perhaps, through art? As Piet Mondrian noted:

> One may observe in art the slow growth towards the Spiritual, while those who produce it remain unaware of this. The conscious path of learning usually leads to the corruption of art. Should these two paths coincide, that is to say that the creator has reached the stage of evolution where conscious, spiritual, direct activity is possible, then one has attained the ideal art..

These are just some of the questions we face, questions that the following memoirs and stories can stir, as we search for meaning and truth. We are a nation of seekers, searching for consciousness to unfold.

Right: Grant Wood, *Parson Weems' Fable.* Parson Mason Locke Weems draws back the curtain to reveal the story of George Washington and the cherry tree. Intellectuals rejected much of American folklore after the Depression, and in this painting the artist seeks to reawaken interest in it. The boy's head is taken from the Gilbert Stuart portrait which also appears on one-dollar bills.

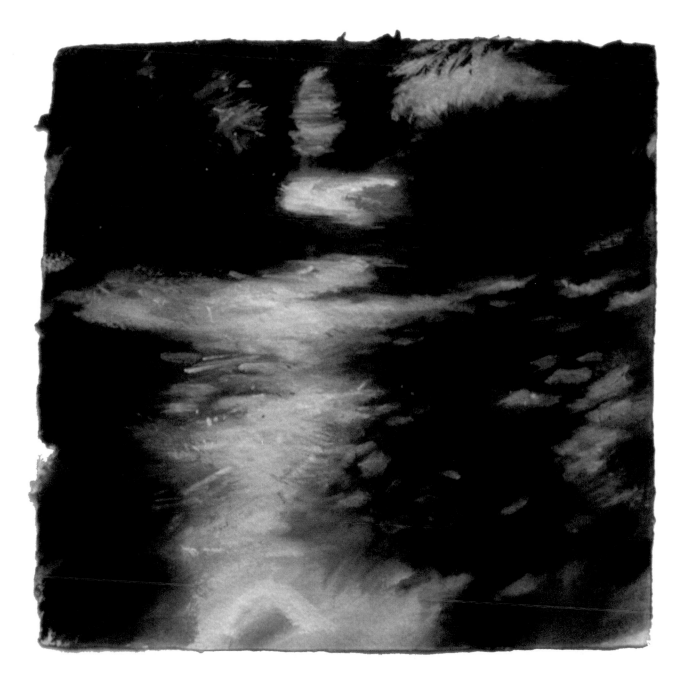

THE ROAD NOT TAKEN

Robert Frost

TWO ROADS DIVERGED IN A YELLOW WOOD,
And sorry I could not travel both
And be one traveler, long I stood
And looked down one as far as I could
To where it bent in the undergrowth;
Then took the other, as just as fair,
And having perhaps the better claim,
Because it was grassy and wanted wear;
Though as for that the passing there
Had worn them really about the same,
And both that morning equally lay
In leaves no step had trodden black.
Oh, I kept the first for another day!
Yet knowing how way leads on to way,
I doubted if I should ever come back.
I shall be telling this with a sigh
Somewhere ages and ages hence:
Two roads diverged in a wood, and I—
I took the one less traveled by,
And that has made all the difference.

Left: Nick Andrew, *Davidea.*

SIDDHARTHA

Herman Hesse

SIDDHARTHA HAD BEGUN TO feel the seeds of discontent within him. He had begun to feel that the love of his father and mother, and also the love of his friend Govinda, would not always make him happy, give him peace, satisfy and suffice him. He had begun to suspect that his worthy father and his other teachers, the wise Brahmins, had already passed on to him the bulk and best of their wisdom, that they had already poured the sum total of their knowledge into his waiting vessel; and the vessel was not full, his intellect was not satisfied, his soul was not at peace, his heart was not still. The ablutions were good, but they were water; they did not wash sins away, they did not relieve the distressed heart. The sacrifices and the supplication of the gods were excellent—but were they everything? Did the sacrifices give happiness? And what about the gods? Was it really Prajapati who had created the world? Was it not Atman, He alone, who had created it? Were not the gods forms created like me and you, mortal, transient? Was it therefore good and right, was it a sensible and worthy act to offer sacrifices to the gods? To whom else should one offer sacrifices, to whom else should one pay honor but to Him, Atman, the Only One? And where was Atman to be found, where did He dwell, where did His eternal heart beat, if not within the Self, in the innermost, in the eternal which each person carried within him? But where was this Self, this innermost? It was not flesh and bone, it was not thought or consciousness. That was what the wise men taught. Where, then, was it? To press towards the Self, towards Atman—was there another way that was worth seeking? Nobody showed the way, nobody knew it—neither his father, nor the teachers and wise men, nor the holy songs. The Brahmins and their holy books knew everything, everything; they had gone into everything—the creation of the world, the origin of speech, food, inhalation, exhalation, the arrangement of the senses, the acts of the gods. They knew a tremendous number of things—but was it worthwhile knowing all these things if they did not know the one important thing, the only important thing?

Many verses of the holy books, above all the Upanishads of SamaVeda, spoke of this innermost thing. It is written: "Your soul is the whole world." It says that when a man is asleep, he penetrates his innermost and dwells

Above: Sarah Pletts, *Buddhist Shrine.*

in Atman. There was wonderful wisdom in these verses; all the knowledge of the sages was told here in enchanting language, pure as honey collected by the bees. No, this tremendous amount of knowledge, collected and preserved by successive generations of wise Brahmins, could not be easily overlooked. But where were the Brahmins, the priests, the wise men, who were successful not only in having this most profound knowledge, but in experiencing it? Where were the initiated who, attaining Atman in sleep, could retain it in consciousness, in life, everywhere, in speech and in action? Siddhartha knew many worthy Brahmins, above all his father—holy, learned, of highest esteem. His father was worthy of admiration; his manner was quiet and noble. He lived a good life, his words were wise; fine and noble thoughts dwelt in his head—but even he who knew so much, did he live in bliss, was he at peace? Was he not also a seeker, insatiable? Did he not go continually to the holy springs with an insatiable thirst, to the sacrifices, to books, to the Brahmins' discourses? Why must he, the blameless one, wash away his sins and endeavor to cleanse himself anew each day? Was Atman then not within him? Was not then the source within his own heart? One must find the source within one' s own Self, one must possess it. Everything else was seeking—a detour, error.

Siddhartha went into the room where his father was sitting on a mat made of bast. He went up behind his father and remained standing there until his father felt his presence. "Is it you, Siddhartha?" the Brahmin asked. "Then speak what is in your mind."

Siddhartha said: "With your permission, Father, I have come to tell you that I wish to leave your house tomorrow and join the ascetics. I wish to become a Samana. I trust my father will not object."

The Brahmin was silent so long that the stars passed across the small window and changed their design before the silence in the room was finally broken. His son stood silent and motionless with his arms folded. The father, silent and motionless, sat on the mat, and the stars passed across the sky. Then his, father said: "It is not seemly for Brahmins to utter forceful and angry words, but there is displeasure in my heart. I should not like to hear you make this request a second time."

The Brahmin rose slowly. Siddhartha remained silent with folded arms.

"Why are you waiting?" asked his father.

"You know why," answered Siddhartha.

His father left the room displeased and lay down on his bed.

As an hour passed by and he could not sleep the Brahmin rose, wandered up and down and then left the house. He looked through the small window, of the room and saw Siddhartha standing there with his arms folded, unmoving. He could see his pale robe shimmering. His heart troubled, the father returned to his bed.

As another hour passed and the Brahmin could not sleep, he rose again, walked up and down, left the house and saw the moon had risen. He looked through the window. Siddhartha stood there unmoving, his arms folded; the moon shone on his bare shinbones. His heart troubled, the father went to bed.

He returned again after an hour and again after two hours, looked through the window and saw Siddhartha standing there. in the moonlight, in the starlight, in the dark. And he came silently again, hour after hour, looked into the room, and saw him standing unmoving. His heart filled with anger, with anxiety, with fear, with sorrow.

And in the last hour of the night, before daybreak, he returned again, entered the room and saw the youth standing there. He seemed tall and a stranger to him.

"Siddhartha," he said, "why are you waiting?"

"You know why."

"Will you go on standing and waiting until it is day, noon, evening?

"I will stand and wait."

"You will grow tired, Siddhartha."

"I will grow tired."

"You will fall asleep, Siddhartha."

"I will not fall asleep."

"You will die, Siddhartha."

"I will die."

"And would you rather die than obey your father?"

"Siddhartha has always obeyed his father."

"So you will give up your project?"

"Siddhartha will do what his father tells him."

The first light of day entered the room. The Brahmin saw that Siddhartha's knees trembled slightly, but there was no trembling in Siddhartha's face; his eyes looked far away. Then the father realized that Siddhartha could no longer remain with him at home—that he had already left him.

The father touched Siddhartha's shoulder.

"You will go into the forest," he said, "and become a Samana. If you find bliss in the forest, come back and teach it to me. If you find disillusionment, come back, and we shall again offer sacrifices to the gods together. Now go, kiss your mother and tell her where you are going. For me, however, it is time to go to the river and perform the first ablution."

He dropped his hand from his son's shoulder and went out. Siddhartha swayed as he tried to walk. He controlled himself, bowed to his father and went to his mother to do what had been told to him.

THERE'S NO PLACE LIKE HOME

L. Frank Baum
Excerpt from *The Wizard of Oz*

DOROTHY WASHED HER FACE AND COMBED HER HAIR, AND THE LION SHOOK THE DUST out of his mane, and the Scarecrow patted himself into his best shape, and the Woodman polished his tin and oiled his joints.

When they were all quite presentable they followed the soldier girl into a big room where the Witch Glinda sat upon a throne of rubies.

She was both beautiful and young to their eyes. Her hair was a rich red in color and fell in flowing ringlets over her shoulders. Her dress was pure white but her eyes were blue, and they looked kindly upon the little girl.

"What can I do for you, my child?" she asked.

Dorothy told the Witch all her story: how the cyclone had brought her to the Land of Oz, how she had found her companions, and of the wonderful adventures they had met with.

Left: Cathryn Chase, *Gateway to Other Worlds*. Just as Dorothy was shifted into another world that helped her to revision the one she lived in, so this artist envisages a portal to somewhere else, existing within a recognizable landscape. "Somewhere else" is only one step away.

"My greatest wish now," she added, "is to get back to Kansas, for Aunt Em will surely think something dreadful has happened to me, and that will make her put on mourning; and unless the crops are better this year than they were last, I am sure Uncle Henry cannot afford it."

Glinda leaned forward and kissed the sweet, upturned face of the loving little girl.

"Bless your dear heart," she said, "I am sure I can tell you of a way to get back to Kansas." Then she added, "But, if I do, you must give me the Golden Cap."

"Willingly!" exclaimed Dorothy; "indeed, it is of no use to me now, and when you have it you can command the Winged Monkeys three times."

"And I think I shall need their service just those three times," answered Glinda, smiling.

Dorothy then gave her the Golden Cap, and the Witch said to the Scarecrow, "What will you do when Dorothy has left us?"

"I will return to the Emerald City," he replied, "for Oz has made me its ruler and the people like me. The only thing that worries me is how to cross the hill of the Hammer-Heads."

"By means of the Golden Cap I shall command the Winged Monkeys to carry you to the gates of the Emerald City," said Glinda, "for it would be a shame to deprive the people of so wonderful a ruler."

"Am I really wonderful?" asked the Scarecrow.

"You are unusual," replied Glinda.

Turning to the Tin Woodman, she asked, "What will become of you when Dorothy leaves this country?"

He leaned on his axe and thought a moment. Then he said, "The Winkies were very kind to me, and wanted me to rule over them after the Wicked Witch died. I am fond of the Winkies, and if I could get back again to the Country of the West, I should like nothing better than to rule over them forever."

"My second command to the Winged Monkeys," said Glinda "will be that they carry you safely to the land of the Winkies. Your brain may not be so large to look at as those of the Scarecrow, but you are really brighter than he is—when you are well polished—and I am sure you will rule the Winkies wisely and well."

Then the Witch looked at the big, shaggy Lion and asked, "When Dorothy has returned to her own home, what will become of you?"

Right: Glinda the Good Witch of the North, played by Billie Burke, and Dorothy Gale, played by Judy Garland, in the 1939 movie, *The Wizard of Oz.*

"Over the hill of the Hammer-Heads," he answered, "lies a grand old forest, and all the beasts that live there have made me their King. If I could only get back to this forest, I would pass my life very happily there."

"My third command to the Winged Monkeys," said Glinda, "shall be to carry you to your forest. Then, having used up the powers of the Golden Cap, I shall give it to the King of the Monkeys, that he and his band may thereafter be free for evermore."

The Scarecrow and the Tin Woodman and the Lion now thanked the Good Witch earnestly for her kindness; and Dorothy exclaimed:

"You are certainly as good as you are beautiful! But you have not yet told me how to get back to Kansas."

"Your Silver Shoes will carry you over the desert," replied Glinda. "If you had known their power you could have gone back to your Aunt Em the very first day you came to this country."

"But then I should not have had my wonderful brains!" cried the Scarecrow. "I might have passed my whole life in the farmer's cornfield."

"And I should not have had my lovely heart," said the Tin Woodman. "I might have stood and rusted in the forest till the end of the world."

"And I should have lived a coward forever," declared the Lion, "and no beast in all the forest would have had a good word to say to me."

"This is all true," said Dorothy, "and I am glad I was of use to these good friends. But now that each of them has had what he most desired, and each is happy in having a kingdom to rule besides, I think I should like to go back to Kansas."

"The Silver Shoes," said the Good Witch, "have wonderful powers. And one of the most curious things about them is that they can carry you to any place in the world in three steps, and each step will be made in the wink of an eye. All you have to do is to knock the heels together three times and command the shoes to carry you wherever you wish to go."

"If that is so," said the child joyfully, "I will ask them to carry me back to Kansas at once."

She threw her arms around the Lion's neck and kissed him, patting his big head tenderly. Then she kissed the Tin Woodman, who was weeping in a way most dangerous to his joints. But she hugged the soft, stuffed body of the Scarecrow in her arms instead of kissing his painted face, and found she was crying herself at this sorrowful parting from her loving comrades.

Glinda the Good stepped down from her ruby throne to give the little girl a good-bye kiss, and Dorothy thanked her for all the kindness she had shown to her friends and herself.

Dorothy now took Toto up solemnly in her arms, and having said one last good-bye she clapped the heels of her shoes together three times, saying:

"Take me home to Aunt Em!"

Instantly she was whirling through the air, so swiftly that all she could see or feel was the wind whistling past her ears.

The Silver Shoes took but three steps, and then she stopped so suddenly that she rolled over upon the grass several times before she knew where she was.

At length, however, she sat up and looked about her.

"Good gracious!" she cried.

For she was sitting on the broad Kansas prairie, and just before her was the new farmhouse Uncle Henry built after the cyclone had carried away the old one. Uncle Henry was milking the cows in the barnyard, and Toto had jumped out of her arms and was running toward the barn, barking furiously.

Dorothy stood up and found she was in her stocking-feet. For the Silver Shoes had fallen off in her flight through the air, and were lost forever in the desert.

Aunt Em had just come out of the house to water the cabbages when she looked up and saw Dorothy running toward her.

"My darling child!" she cried, folding the little girl in her arms and covering her face with kisses.

"Where in the world did you come from?"

"From the Land of Oz," said Dorothy gravely. "And here is Toto, too. And oh, Aunt Em! I'm so glad to be at home again!"

A CITY OF CHURCHES

Donald Barthelme

Y es," Mr. Phillips said, "ours is a city of churches all right." Cecelia
nodded, following his pointing hand. Both sides of the street were
solidly lined with churches, standing shoulder to shoulder in a
variety of architectural styles. The Bethel Baptist stood next to the Holy Messiah
Free Baptist, Saint Paul's Episcopal next to Grace Evangelical Covenant. Then

Right: Lyonel Feininger, *Church of Heiligenhafen.* In the painting the church tower appears in a setting that could be either real or illusory. The nature of the painting also demonstrates the artist's sense of order in the world. The accompanying story is set in an identifiable, yet obviously fantastic world, where the sense of harmonious order shown in this painting has been exaggerated into something destructive.

came the first Christian Science, the Church of God, All Souls, Our Lady of Victory, the Society of Friends, the Assembly of God, and the Church of the Holy Apostles. The spires and steeples of the traditional buildings were jammed in next to the broad imaginative flights of the "contemporary" designs.

"Everyone here take a great interest in church matters," Mr. Phillips said.

Will I fit in, Cecelia wondered. She had come to Prester to open a branch office of a car-rental concern.

"I'm not especially religious," she said to Mr. Phillips, who was in the real-estate business.

"Not *now*," he answered. "Not *yet*. But we have many fine young people here. You'll get integrated into the community soon enough. The immediate problem is where are you to live? Most people," he said, "live in the church of their choice. All of our churches have many extra rooms. I have a few belfry apartments that I can show you. What price range were you thinking of?"

They turned a corner and were confronted with more churches. They passed Saint Luke's, the Church of the Epiphany, All Saints Ukrainian Orthodox, Saint Clement's, Fountain Baptist, Union Congregational, Saint Anargyri's, Temple Emanuel, the First Church of Christ Reformed. The mouths of all the churches were gaping open. Inside lights could be seen dimly.

"I can go up to a hundred and ten," Cecelia said. "Do you have nay buildings here that are *not* churches?"

"None," said Mr. Phillips. "Of course, many of our fine church structures also do double duty as something else." He indicated a handsome Georgian façade. "That one" he said, "houses the United Methodist and the Board of Education. The one next to it, which is the Antioch Pentecostal, has the barbershop."

It was true. A red-and-white striped barber pole was attached inconspicuously to the front of the Antioch Pentecostal.

"Do many people rent cars here?" Cecelia asked. "Or would they, if there was a handy place to rent them?"

"Oh, I don't know," said Mr. Phillips. "Renting a car implies that you want to go somewhere. Most people are pretty content right here. We have a lot of activities. I don't think I'd pick the car-rental business if I was just starting out in Prester. But you'll do fine." He showed her a small, extremely modern building with a severe brick, steel, and glass front. "That's Saint Barnabas. Nice bunch of people over there. Wonderful spaghetti suppers."

Cecelia could see a number of heads looking out of the windows. But when they saw that she was staring at them, the heads disappeared.

"Do you think it's healthy for so many churches to be gathered together in one place?" she asked her guide. "It doesn't seem . . . *balanced,* if you know what I mean."

"We are famous for our churches," Mr. Phillips replied. "They are harmless. Here we are now."

He opened a door and they began climbing many flights of dusty stairs. At the end of the climb they entered a good-sized room, square, with windows on all four sides. There was a bed, a table and two chairs, lamps, a rug. Four very large brass bells hung in the exact center of the room.

"What a view!" Mr. Phillips exclaimed. "Come here and look."

"Do they actually ring these bells?" Cecelia asked.

"Three times a day," Mr. Phillips said, smiling. "Morning, noon, and night. Of course when they're rung you have to be pretty quick at getting out of the way. You get hit in the head by one of these babies and that's all she wrote."

"God Almighty," said Cecelia involuntarily. Then she said, "Nobody lives in the belfry apartments. That's why they're empty."

"You think so?" Mr. Phillips said.

"You can only rent them to new people in town," she said accusingly.

"I wouldn't do that," MR. Phillips said. "It would go against the spirit of Christian fellowship."

"This town is a little creepy, you know that?"

"That may be, but it's not for you to say, is it? I mean, you're new here. You should walk cautiously, for a while. If you don't want an upper apartment, I have a basement over at Central Presbyterian. You'd have to share it. Three are two women in there now."

"I don't want to share," Cecelia said. "I want a place of my own."

"Why?" the real-estate man asked curiously. "For what purpose?"

"Purpose?" asked Cecelia. "There is no particular purpose. I just want"

"That's not usual here. Most people live with other people. Husbands and wives. Sons with their mothers. People have roommates. That's the usual pattern."

"Still, I prefer a place of my own."

"It's very unusual."

"Do you have any such places? Besides bell towers, I mean?"

"I guess there are a few," Mr. Phillips said, with clear reluctance. "I can show you one or two, I suppose."

He paused for a moment.

"It's just that we have different values, maybe, from some of the surrounding communities," he explained. "We've been written up a lot. We have four minutes on the 'CBS Evening News' one time. Three or four years ago. 'A City of Churches,' it was called."

"Yes, a place of my own is essential," Cecelia said, "if I am to survive here."

"That's kind of a funny attitude to take," Mr. Phillips said. "What denomination are you?"

Cecelia was silent. The truth was, she wasn't anything.

"I said, what denomination are you?" Mr. Phillips repeated.

"I can will my dreams," Cecelia said. "I can dream whatever I want. If I want to dream that I'm having a good time, in Paris or some other city, all I have to do is go to sleep and I will dream that dream. I can dream whatever I want."

"What do you dream, then, mostly?" Mr. Phillips said, looking at her closely.

"Mostly sexual things," she said. She was not afraid of him.

"Prester is not that kind of a town," Mr. Phillips said, looking away.

T he doors of the churches were opening, on both sides of the street. Small groups of people came out and stood there, in front of the churches, gazing at Cecelia and Mr. Phillips.

A young man stepped forward and shouted, *"Everyone in this town already has a car! There is no one in this town who doesn't have a car!"*

"Is that true?" Cecelia asked Mr. Phillips.

"Yes," he said. "It's true. No one would rent a car here. Not in a hundred years."

"Then I won't stay," she said. "I'll go somewhere else."

"You must stay," he said. "There is already a car-rental office for you. In Mount Moriah Baptist, on the lobby floor. There is a counter and a telephone and a rack of car keys. And a calendar."

"I won't stay," she said. "Not if there's not any sound business reason for staying."

"We want you," said Mr. Phillips. "We want you standing behind the counter of the car-rental agency, during regular business hours. It will make the town complete."

"I won't," she said. "Not me."

"You must. It's essential."

"I'll dream," she said. "Things you won't like."

"We are discontented," said Mr. Phillips. "Terribly, terribly discontented. Something is wrong."

"I'll dream the Secret," she said. "You'll be sorry."

"We are like other towns, except that we are perfect," he said. "Our discontent can only be held in check by perfection. We need a car-rental girl. Someone must stand behind that counter."

"I'll dream the life you are most afraid of," Cecelia threatened.

"You are ours," he said, gripping her arm. "Our car-rental girl. Be nice. There is nothing you can do."

"Wait and see," Cecelia said.

S I N N E R S   I N   T H E   H A N D S
O F   A N   A N G R Y   G O D

Jonathan Edwards, July 8, 1741

T HAT WORLD OF MISERY, THAT LAKE OF BURNING BRIMSTONE, IS EXTENDED abroad under you. There is the dreadful pit of the glowing flames of the wrath of God; there is hell's wide gaping mouth open; and you have nothing to stand upon, nor any thing to take hold of, there is nothing between you and hell but the air; it is only the power and mere pleasure of God that holds you up.

You probably are not sensible of this; you find you are kept out of hell, but do not see the hand of God in it; but look at other things, as the good

Right: Robert Gwathmey, *Belle*. In this critical painting of Southern archetypes, religion, ignorance, and superstition are expressed within many symbols to create a tragic world of madness. This is reflected within the extreme rhetoric of the words of the accompanying sermon.

state of your bodily constitution, your care of your own life, and the means you use for your own preservation. But indeed these things are nothing; if God should withdraw his band, they would avail no more to keep you from falling, than the thin air to hold up a person that is suspended in it.

Your wickedness makes you as it were heavy as lead, and to tend downwards with great weight and pressure towards hell; and if God should let you go, you would immediately sink and swiftly descend and plunge into the bottomless gulf, and your healthy constitution, and your own care and prudence, and best contrivance, and all your righteousness, would have no more influence to uphold you and keep you out of hell, than a spider's web would have to stop a falling rock. Were it not for the sovereign pleasure of God, the earth would not bear you one moment; for you are a burden to it; the creation groans with you; the creature is made subject to the bondage of your corruption, not willingly; the sun does not willingly shine upon you to give you light to serve sin and Satan; the earth does not willingly yield her increase to satisfy your lusts; nor is it willingly a stage for your wickedness to be acted upon; the air does not willingly serve you for breath to maintain the flame of life in your vitals, while you spend your life in the service of God's enemies. God's creatures are good, and were made for men to serve God with, and do not willingly subserve to any other purpose, and groan when they are abused to purposes so directly contrary to their nature and end. And the world would spew

Left: Jack Levine, *The Visit From The Second World.* Jack Levine is noted for his paintings of powerful figures such as gangsters, politicians, and generals in actions that are laden with ironic overtones. This painting contains a double irony. Levine saw this procession in Jerusalem in the 1970s and was initially struck by the central figure—the Metropolitan—later to become the Patriarch of the Russian Orthodox Church, wearing mirrored sunglasses like a Miami Beach tourist. He learned that the Metropolitan was in Jerusalem to take over deeds of property from the White Russians. Levine felt the irony of a representative of the Soviet Union acquiring land, not through military aggression, but through legal means.

you out, were it not for the sovereign hand of him who hath subjected it in hope. There are black clouds of God's wrath now hanging directly over your heads, full of the dreadful storm, and big with thunder; and were it not for the restraining hand of God, it would immediately burst forth upon you. The sovereign pleasure of God, for the present, stays his rough wind; otherwise it would come with fury, and your destruction would come like a whirlwind, and you would be like the chaff of the summer threshing floor.

The wrath of God is like great waters that are dammed for the present; they increase more and more, and rise higher and higher, till an outlet is given; and the longer the stream is stopped, the more rapid and mighty is its course, when once it is let loose. It is true, that judgment against your evil works has not been executed hitherto; the floods of God's vengeance have been withheld; but your guilt in the mean time is constantly increasing, and you are every day treasuring up more wrath; the waters are constantly rising, and waxing more and more mighty; and there is nothing but the mere pleasure of God, that holds the waters back, that are unwilling to be stopped, and press hard to go forward. If God should only withdraw his hand from the flood-gate, it would immediately fly open, and the fiery floods of the fierceness and wrath of God, would rush forth with inconceivable fury, and would come upon you with omnipotent power; and if your strength were ten thousand times greater than it is, yea, ten thousand times greater than the strength of the stoutest, sturdiest devil in hell, it would be nothing to withstand or endure it . . .

All you that were never born again, and made new creatures, and raised from being dead in sin, to a state of new, and before altogether unexperienced light and life, are in the hands of an angry God. However you may have reformed your life in many things, and may have had religious affections, and may keep up a form of religion in your families and closets, and in the house of God, it is nothing but his mere pleasure that keeps you

No, he could not believe. He had seen for himself. It was there, in the city, in all the godlessness, the eyes of the whores, the men at cards, the sleeping fat man, and the mad headlines, it was all there, unbelief, ungodliness, everywhere, all the world forgetting. How could he believe?

—William Saroyan

from being this moment swallowed up in everlasting destruction. However unconvinced you may now be of the truth of what you hear, by and by you will be fully convinced of it. Those that are gone from being in the like circumstances with you, see that it was so with them; for destruction came suddenly upon most of them; when they expected nothing of it, and while they were saying, Peace and safety: now they see, that those things on which they depended for peace and safety, were nothing but thin air and empty shadows.

The God that holds you over the pit of hell, much as one holds a spider, or some loathsome insect over the fire, abhors you, and is dreadfully provoked: his wrath towards you bums like fire; he looks upon you as worthy of nothing else, but to be cast into the fire; he is of purer eyes than to bear to have you in his sight; you are ten thousand times more abominable in his eyes, than the most hateful venomous serpent is in ours. You have offended him infinitely more than ever a stubborn rebel did his prince; and yet it is nothing but his hand that holds you from falling into the fire every moment. It is to be ascribed to nothing else, that you did not go to hell the last night; that you was suffered to awake again in this world, after you closed your eyes to sleep. And there is no other reason to be given, why you have not dropped into hell since you arose in the morning, but that God's hand has held you up. There is no other reason to be given why you have not gone to hell, since you have sat here in the house of God, provoking his pure eyes by your sinful wicked manner of attending his solemn worship. Yea, there is nothing else that is to be given as a reason why you do not this very moment drop down into hell.

O sinner! Consider the fearful danger you are in: it is a great furnace of wrath, a wide and bottomless pit, full of the fire of wrath, that you are held over in the hand of that God, whose wrath is provoked and incensed as much against you, as against many of the damned in hell. You hang by a slender thread, with the flames of divine wrath flashing about it, and ready every moment to singe it, and bum it asunder; and you have no interest in any Mediator, and nothing lay hold of to save yourself, nothing to keep off the flames of wrath, nothing of your own, nothing that you ever have done, nothing that you can do, to induce God to spare you one moment.

BROTHER JAKE AND THE PREACHER

Lorraine Johnson-Coleman

ROTHER JAKE LOOKED UP AT THE HEAVENS AND wondered if the Lord was looking down at him. He could be sure the Devil was looking up at him—that rascal seemed to be everywhere he was all of the time. No, it was the Lord that worried him. God just had to be looking, thought Brother Jake nervously, so that He could see that Jake was really here. Brother Jake needed all the points he could collect, and it wasn't too often that he came by for a visit, so if God wasn't looking today, there would be no telling when He would see Brother Jake this way again. Heavens, these seats were hard, this suit was too tight, and these shoes hurt like hell! Oops, was it a sin to be thinkin' hell, or was it all right as long as you didn't say it out loud? Brother Jake couldn't afford to be committing no wrongs, especially not in the church. He was here to be adding to the tally, not to be takin' nothin' away! Seemed like sittin' through this old lousy service ought to give a body a few bonus points. These folks singing didn't sound nothing like he'd remembered, and the preacher couldn't preach a lick! The Reverend wasn't hittin' on nothin', nothin' at all. A whole lot of big words and even more supposin'. Supposin' this and supposin' that. Suppose he just sat his black butt down? Now suppose that?

Why couldn't these fancy-dancy preachers just come on out and hit it straight, even if they got to use them a crooked stick? This man had to be new. He wasn't around the last time, Brother Jake was sure about that. 'Course that had been 'bout ten years ago, and a whole lot of folks done come and gone since then. Well, it didn't matter how bad it all was, this was where he needed to be. Time was passing on by, and he was getting old fast. It was more than a notion that it was time for him to be gettin' close to the Lord. He would need to be somewhere near Him if he was gonna get to Heaven—sure couldn't get there no other way, and that was exactly where he

Left: James Van Der Zee, *Daddy Grace at the Altar with Choir.*

wanted to go. His mama was expectin' him to show up there sooner or later, and didn't no real man let down his mama, and Lord knew, too, that he'd already been to hell, and he sure wasn't lookin' to go there no more. Hell no! There was still a chance, though, that he'd be able to wrangle him a blessing here today, if only this preacher would say a little something he could grab on to. He wasn't going to worry yet, though, the service wasn't but half over!

Why couldn't that preacher up there preach him one of them sermons like Reverend Cole used to? Now that was a preaching man! If Brother Jake could just get something out of this here message, maybe then he'd have a prayer for getting into Heaven. This was one time somebody ought to shoot the messenger! Now if Reverend Cole had been up there, he would have made sure that Brother Jake got to where he needed to go. That man sure knew 'bout this Heaven and Hell thing, broke it down one time so everybody could see their way clear through. That sure was some sermon Reverend Cole preached that Sunday 'bout ten years ago. It was a lot better than this here. Yessirree, that was some sermon, some sermon indeed.

. . . *Brothers, sisters, saints and sinners, you listening this morning to the words of the Lord as they pass through me, the Reverend James Cole, Sister Sue's baby boy. Today I'm gonna preach on the beautifulness of Heaven and the ugliness of Hell, and I suggest you listen up so you'll know what kind of a fix you might be in. Now I ain't figuring on being so late today that you rot where you sit, but I ain't fixing to short change the Lord, neither.*

Now, 'bout this Heaven and Hell, there's a few things you needs to be understanding. Ya'll know if you look around you that all flesh ain't the same. You got the flesh of the whites and the flesh of the coloreds, and they different as different can be. Well, Heaven and Hell is set up the same way.

The Lord was pretty smart when it come to these things. That's why He ain't made the Heavens and the Hells exactly alike. He made a different Heaven and a different Hell for the different kinds of folks that live on this Earth. That way won't no one place get too crowded and there won't be no mixing of the races. So all of you coloreds who was figuring on breaking holy bread with the whites - there ain't gonna be none of that, so don't even be figuring on it. You ought to know that the white folks wouldn't be studying on nothing like that, and 'sides, the way they cook, you ain't gonna want none of their grub no way, and their music—Lord, have mercy, we ain't even gonna speak on that!

Now, our New Jerusalem ain't gonna be no coon town. No barbecues, fish frys, or Saturday-night frolics, but they'll be plenty of good food and time to take a rest. But some of ya'll ain't gonna get in 'less you stop your evil ways. When death comes knocking your gonna miss that train to glory. You can roll your eyes, stomp your feet, and poke out your lips all you want to, but it ain't gonna do you a bit of good. It won't get you nowhere except that place called "Hell" that stays about fifty below.

Yeah, that's the place you going if you don't do right—a place that freezes over all year long. A place where the Devil gonna say good morning by knocking you upside your head with snowballs. Now you think on that, you no-good, sin-filled benchwarmers. It's gonna be so cold that it's gonna freeze your lips shut! You ain't gonna be able to talk, not one word—that's torture for some of ya'all. You just remember this:

It rains and it hails.
Snow coming down like the Devil poured it from a pail.
But it's way too late to weep or cry 'cause
the preacher told me this was where I'd be when I die . . .

Brother Jake remembered that sermon word for word. The best part came long after everybody was gone. He went up to Reverend Cole and asked him, " What kind of Heaven and Hell was you preaching 'bout, Reverend? I ain't never heard nothing like that before."

"Oh, Brother Jake, you know that I knows that the Bible says Hell is fire and brimstone, but then you know, too, that you can't be scaring no colored folks with hot weather. If you wants to get to 'em, then you got to be scaring them with freezing cold." And with that, Reverend Cole chuckled his way past Brother Jake and walked right out the door.

Brother Jake looked up at this here Reverend Jackson who was still struggling to make a point. It looked like there wasn't going to be a chance for him to earn his place in Heaven here today. He smiled as he thought about Reverend Cole again. No, they sure don't make 'em like that no more. No, they sure as hell don't!

THE PROBLEM OF OLD HARJO

John M. Oskison

THE SPIRIT OF THE LORD HAD DESCENDED UPON OLD HARJO. FROM THE NEW MISSIONARY, JUST OUT FROM New York, he had learned that he was a sinner. The fire in the new missionary's eyes and her gracious appeal had convinced old Harjo that this was the time to repent and be saved. He was very much in earnest and he assured Miss Evans that he wanted to be baptized and received into the church at once. Miss Evans was enthusiastic and went to Mrs. Rowell with the news. It was Mrs. Rowell who had said that it was no use to try to convert the older Indians, and she, after fifteen years of work in Indian Territory missions, should have known. Miss Evans was pardonably proud of her conquest.

"Old Harjo converted!" exclaimed Mrs. Rowell. "Dear Miss Evans, do you know that old Harjo has two wives?" To the older woman it was as if someone had said to her "Madame, the Sultan of Turkey wishes to teach one of your mission Sabbath school classes."

"But," protested the younger woman, "he is really sincere, and—"

Right: Marsden Hartley, *American Indian Symbols.* Hartley, an American artist, painted this in Germany after seeing a collection of American Indian artifacts in the Berlin Ethnographic Museum. This is part of his "Amerika" series conceived as a fusion of German expressionism, Cubism, Hartley's own spirituality, and a new interest in Native American culture. Whilst the painting is a successful blend of what could have been disparate ideas, no resolution is found to the cultural conflict in the story.

"Then ask him," Mrs. Rowell interrupted a bit sternly, "if he will put away one of his wives. Ask him, before he comes into the presence of the Lord, if he is willing to conform to the laws of the country in which he lives, the country that guarantees his idle existence. Miss Evans, your work is not even begun." No one who knew Mrs. Rowell would say that she lacked sincerity and patriotism. Her own cousin was an earnest crusader against Mormonism, and had gathered a goodly share of that wagonload of protests that the Senate had been asked to read when it was considering whether a certain statesman of Utah should be allowed to represent his state at Washington.

In her practical, tactful way, Mrs. Rowell had kept clear of such embarrassments. At first she had written letters of indignant protest to the Indian Office against the toleration of bigamy amongst the tribes. A wise inspector had been sent to the mission, and this man had pointed out that it was better to ignore certain things, "deplorable, to be sure," than to attempt to make over the habits of the old men. Of course, the young Indians would not be permitted to take more than one wife each.

So Mrs. Rowell had discreetly limited her missionary efforts to the young, and had exercised toward the old and bigamous only that strict charity which even a hopeless sinner might claim.

Miss Evans, it was to be regretted, had only the vaguest notions about "expediency"; so weak on matters of doctrine was she that the news that Harjo was flying with two wives didn't startle her. She was young and possessed of but one enthusiasm—that for saving souls.

"I suppose," she ventured, "that old Harjo *must* put away one wife before he can join the church."

"There can be no question about it, Miss Evans."

"Then I shall have to ask him to do it." Miss Evans regretted the necessity for forcing this sacrifice, but had no doubt that the Indian would make it in order to accept the gift of salvation which she was commissioned to bear to him.

Harjo lived in a "double" log cabin three miles from the mission. His ten acres of corn had been gathered into its fence-rail crib; four hogs that were to furnish his winter's bacon had been brought in from the woods and penned conveniently near to the crib; out in a corner of the garden, a fat mound of dirt rose where the crop of turnips and potatoes had been buried against the corrupting frost; and in the hayloft of his log stable were stored many pumpkins, dried corn, onions (suspended in bunches from the rafters) and the varied forage that Mrs. Harjo number one and Mrs. Harjo number two had thriftily provided. Three cows, three young heifers, two colts, and two patient, capable mares bore the Harjo brand, a fantastic "HH" that the old man had designed.

Materially, Harjo was solvent; and if the Government had ever come to his aid he could not recall the date.

This attempt to rehabilitate old Harjo morally, Miss Evans felt, was not one to be made at the mission; it should be undertaken in the Creek's own home, where the evidences of his sin should confront him as she explained.

When Miss Evans rode up to the block in front of Harjo's cabin, the old Indian came out, slowly and with a broadening smile of welcome on his face. A clean gray flannel shirt had taken the place of the white collarless garment, with crackling stiff bosom that he had worn to the mission meetings. Comfortable, well-patched moccasins had been substituted for creaking boots, and brown corduroys, belted in at the waist, for tight black trousers. His abundant gray hair fell down on his shoulders. In his eyes, clear and large and black, glowed the light of true hospitality. Miss Evans thought of the patriarchs as she saw him lead her horse out to the stable; thus Abraham might have looked and lived.

"Harjo," began Miss Evans before following the old man to the covered passageway between the disconnected cabins, "is it true that you have two wives?" Her tone was neither stern nor accusatory. The Creek had heard that question before, from scandalized missionaries and perplexed registry clerks when he went to Muscogee to enroll himself and his family in one of the many "final" records ordered to be made by the government preparatory to dividing the Creek lands among the individual citizens.

For answer, Harjo called, first into the cabin that was used as a kitchen and then, in a loud, clear voice, toward the small field, where Miss Evans saw a flock of half-grown turkeys running about in the corn stubble. From the kitchen emerged a tall, thin Indian woman of fifty-five, with a red handkerchief bound severely over her head. She spoke to Miss Evans and sat down in the passageway. Presently, a clear, sweet voice was heard in the field; a stout, handsome woman, about the same age as the other, climbed the rail fence and came up to the house. She, also, greeted Miss Evans briefly. Then she carried a tin basin to the well nearby, where she filled it to the brim. Setting it down on the horse block, she rolled back her sleeves, tucked in the collar of her gray blouse, and plunged her face in the water. In a minute she came out of the kitchen freshened and smiling. 'Liza Harjo had been pulling dried bean stalks at one end of the field, and it was dirty work. At last old Harjo turned to Miss Evans and said, "These two my wife—this one 'Liza, this one Jennie."

It was done with simple dignity. Miss Evans bowed and stammered. Three pairs of eyes were turned upon her in patient, courteous inquiry.

It was hard to state the case. The old man was so evidently proud of his women, and so flattered by Miss Evans' interest in them, that he would find it hard to understand. Still, it had to be done, and Miss Evans took the plunge.

"Harjo, you want to come into our church?" The old man's face lighted.

"Oh, yes, I would come to Jesus, please, my friend."

"Do you know, Harjo, that the Lord commanded that one man should mate with but one woman?" The question was stated again in simpler terms, and the Indian replied, "Me know that now, my friend. Long time ago"—Harjo plainly meant the whole period previous to his conversion—"me did not know. The Lord Jesus did not speak to me in that time and so I was blind. I do what blind man do."

"Harjo, you must have only one wife when you come into our church. Can't you give up one of these women?" Miss Evans glanced at the two, sitting by with smiles of polite interest on their faces, understanding nothing. They had not shared Harjo's enthusiasm either for the white man's God or his language.

"Give up my wife?" A sly smile stole over his face. He leaned closer to Miss Evans. "You tell me, my friend, which one I give up." He glanced from 'Liza to Jennie as if to weigh their attractions, and the two rewarded him with their pleasantest smiles. "You tell me which one," he urged.

"Why, Harjo, how can I tell you!" Miss Evans had little sense of humor; she had taken the old man seriously.

"Then," Harjo sighed, continuing the comedy, for surely the missionary was jesting with him, " 'Liza and Jennie must say." He talked to the Indian women for a time, and they laughed heartily. 'Liza, pointing to the other, shook her head. At length Harjo explained, "My friend, they cannot say. Jennie, she would run a race to see which one stay, but 'Liza, she say no, she is fat and cannot run."

Miss Evans comprehended at last. She flushed angrily, and protested, "Harjo, you are making a mock of a sacred subject; I cannot allow you to talk like this."

"But did you not speak in fun, my friend?" Harjo queried, sobering. "Surely you have just said what your friend, the white woman at the mission (he meant Mrs. Rowell) would say, and you do not mean what you say."

"Yes, Harjo, I mean it. It is true that Mrs. Rowell raised the point first, but I agree with her. The church cannot be defiled by receiving a bigamist into its membership." Harjo saw that the young woman was serious, distressingly serious. He was silent for a long time, but at last he raised his head and spoke quietly, "It is not good to talk like that if it is not in fun."

He rose and went to the stable. As he led Miss Evans' horse up to the block it was champing a mouthful of corn, the last of a generous portion that Harjo had put before it. The Indian held the bridle and waited for Miss Evans to mount. She was embarrassed, humiliated, angry. It was absurd to be dismissed in this way by—"by an ignorant old bigamist!" Then the humor of it burst upon her, and its human aspect. In her anxiety concerning the spiritual welfare of the sinner Harjo, she had insulted the man Harjo. She began to understand why Mrs. Rowell had said that the old Indians were hopeless.

"Harjo," she begged, coming out of the passageway, "please forgive me. I do not want you to give up one of your wives. just tell me why you took them."

"I will tell you that, my friend." The old Creek looped the reins over his arm and sat down on the block. "For thirty years Jennie has lived with me as my wife. She is of the Bear people, and she came to me when I was thirty-five and she was twenty-five. She could not come before, for her mother was old, very old, and Jennie, she stay with her and feed her.

"So, when I was thirty years old I took 'Liza for my woman. She is of the Crow people. She help me make this little farm here when there was no farm for many miles around.

"Well, five years 'Liza and me, we live here and work hard. But there was no child. Then the old mother of Jennie she died, and Jennie got no family left in this part of the country. So 'Liza say to me, 'Why don't you take Jennie in here?' I say, 'You don't care?' and she say, 'No, maybe we have children here then.' But we have no children—never have children. We do not like that, but God He would not let it be. So, we have lived here thirty years very happy. Only just now you make me sad."

"Harjo," cried Miss Evans, "forget what I said. Forget that you wanted to join the church." For a young mission worker with a single purpose always before her, Miss Evans was saying a strange thing. Yet she couldn't help saying it; all of her zeal seemed to have been dissipated by a simple statement of the old man.

"I cannot forget to love Jesus, and I want to be saved." Old Harjo spoke with solemn earnestness. The situation was distracting. On one side stood a convert eager for the protection of the church, asking only that he be allowed to fulfill the obligations of humanity and on the other stood the church, represented by Mrs. Rowell, that set an impossible condition on receiving old Harjo to itself. Miss Evans wanted to cry; prayer, she felt, would be entirely inadequate as a means of expression.

"Oh! Harjo," she cried out, "I don't know what to do. I must think it over and talk with Mrs. Rowell again."

But Mrs. Rowell could suggest no way out; Miss Evans' talk with her only gave the older woman another opportunity to preach the folly of wasting time on the old and "unreasonable" Indians. Certainly the church could not listen even to a hint of a compromise in this case. If Harjo wanted to be saved, there was one way and only one—unless—

"Is either of the two women old? I mean, so old that she is—an—"

"Not at all," answered Miss Evans. "They're both strong and—yes, happy. I think they will outlive Harjo."

"Can't you appeal to one of the women to go away? I dare say we could provide for her." Miss Evans, incongruously, remembered Jennie's jesting proposal to race for the right to stay with Harjo. What could the mission provide as a substitute for the little home that 'Liza had helped to create there in the edge of the woods? What other home would satisfy Jennie?

"Mrs. Rowell, are you sure that we ought to try to take one of Harjo's women from him? I'm not sure that it would in the least advance morality amongst the tribe, but I'm certain that it would make three gentle people unhappy for the rest of their lives."

"You may he right, Miss Evans." Mrs. Rowell was not seeking to create unhappiness, for enough of it inevitably came to be pictured in the little mission building. "You may be right," she repeated, "but it is a grievous misfortune that old Harjo should wish to unite with the church."

No one was more regular in his attendance at the mission meetings than old Harjo. Sitting well

Left: Georgia O'Keeffe, *Black Cross, New Mexico.* The black cross dominates a lively and mellow landscape.

forward, he was always in plain view of Miss Evans at the organ. Before the service began, and after it was over the old man greeted the young woman. There was never a spoken question, but in the Creek's eyes was always a mute inquiry.

Once Miss Evans ventured to write to her old pastor in New York, and explain her trouble. This was what he wrote in reply: "I am surprised that you are troubled, for I should have expected you to rejoice, as I do, over this new and wonderful evidence of the Lord's reforming power. Though the church cannot receive the old man so long as he is confessedly a bigamist and violator of his country's just laws, you should be greatly strengthened in your work through bringing him to desire salvation."

"Oh! it's easy to talk when you're free from responsibility!" cried out Miss Evans. "But I woke him up to a desire for this water of salvation that he cannot take. I have seen Harjo's home, and I know how cruel and useless it would he to urge him to give up what he loves—for he does love those two women who have spent half their lives and more with him. What, what can be done?"

Month after month, as old Harjo continued to occupy his seat in the mission meetings, with that mute appeal in his. eyes and a persistent light of hope on his face, Miss Evans repeated the question, "What can be done?" If she was sometimes tempted to say to the old man, "Stop worrying about your soul; you'll get to Heaven as surely as any of us," there was always Mrs. Rowell to remind her that she was not a Mormon missionary. She could not run away from her perplexity. If she should secure a transfer to another station, she felt that Harjo would give up coming to the meetings, and in his despair become a positive influence for evil amongst his people. Mrs. Rowell would not waste her energy on an obstinate old man. No, Harjo was her creation, her impossible convert, and throughout the years, until death—the great solvent which is not always a solvent—came to one of them, would continue to haunt her.

And meanwhile, what?

I DON'T WRITE TO GOD NO MORE

Alice Walker
Excerpt from *The Color Purple*

DEAR NETTIE,
I DON'T WRITE TO GOD NO MORE, I write to you.

What happen to God? ast Shug.

Who that? I say.

She look at me serious.

Big a devil as you is, I say, you not worried bout no God, surely.

She say, Wait a minute. Hold on just a minute here. Just because I don't harass it like some peoples us know don't mean I ain't got religion.

What God do for me? I ast.

She say, Celie! Like she shock. He gave you life, good health, and a good woman that love you to death.

Yeah, I say, and he give me a

Left: Audrey Flack, *Bounty*. The very female viewpoint of this story is echoed by the feeling of abundance in this painting, also by a woman artist. Flack is at the forefront of a 1970s movement called Photo Realism and here she uses paint and canvas to create the illusion of photography. Shug sees God as abundance, "God love everything you loves—and a mess of stuff you don't."

lynched daddy, a crazy mama, a lowdown dog of a step pa and a sister I probably won't ever see again. Anyhow, I say, the God I been praying and writing to is a man. And act just like all the other mens I know. Trifling, forgitful and lowdown.

She say, Miss Celie, You better hush. God might hear you.

Let 'im hear me, I say. If he ever listened to poor colored women the world would be a different place, I can tell you.

She talk and she talk, trying to budge me way from blasphemy. But I blaspheme much as I want to.

All my life I never care what people thought bout nothing I did, I say. But deep in my heart I care about God. What he going to think. And come to find out, he don't think. Just sit up there glorying in being deef, I reckon. But it ain't easy, trying to do without God. Even if you know he ain't there, trying to do without him is a strain.

I is a sinner, say Shug. Cause I was born. I don't deny it. But once you find out what's out there waiting for us, what else can you be?

Sinners have more good times, I say.

You know why? she ast.

Cause you ain't all the time worrying bout God, I say.

Naw, that ain't it, she say. Us worry bout God a lot. But once us feel loved by God, us do the best us can to please him with what us like.

You telling me God love you, and you ain't never done nothing for him? I mean, not go to church, sing in the choir, feed the preacher and all like that?

But if God love me, Celie, I don't have to do all that. Unless I want to. There's a lot of other things I can do that I speck God likes.

Like what? I ast.

Oh, she say. I can lay back and just admire stuff. Be happy. Have a good time.

Well, this sound like blasphemy sure nuff.

She say, Celie, tell the truth, have you ever found God in church? I never did. I just found a bunch of folks hoping for him to show. Any God I ever felt in church I brought in with me. And I think all the other folks did too. They come to church to share God, not find God.

Some folks didn't have him to share, I said. They the ones didn't speak to me while I was there struggling with my big belly and Mr. —— children.

Right, she say.

Then she say: Tell me what your God look like, Celie.

Aw naw, I say. I'm too shame. Nobody ever ast me this before, so I'm sort of took by surprise. Besides, when I think about it, it don't seem quite right. But it all I got. I decide to stick up for him, just to see what Shug say.

Okay, I say. He big and old and tall and graybearded and white. He wear white robes and go barefooted.

Blue eyes? she ast.

Sort of bluish-gray. Cool. Big though. White lashes, I say.

She laugh.

Why you laugh? I ast. I don't think it so funny. What you expect him to look like, Mr. —— ?

That wouldn't be no improvement, she say. Then she tell me this old white man is the same God she used to see when she prayed. If you wait to find God in church, Celie, she say, that's who is bound to show up, cause that's where he live.

How come? I ast.

Cause that's the one that's in the white folks' white bible.

Shug! I say. God wrote the bible, white folks had nothing to do with it.

How come he look just like them, then? she say. Only bigger? And a heap more hair. How come the bible just like everything else they make, all about them doing one thing and another, and all the colored folks doing is gitting cursed?

I never thought bout that.

Nettie say somewhere in the bible it say Jesus' hair was like lamb's wool, I say.

Well, say Shug, if he came to any of these churches we talking bout he'd have to have it conked before anybody paid him any attention. The last thing niggers want to think about they God is that his hair kinky.

That's the truth, I say.

Ain't no way to read the bible and not think God white, she say. Then she sigh. When I found out I thought God was white, and a man, I lost interest. You mad cause he don't seem to listen to your prayers. Humph! Do the mayor listen to anything colored say? Ask Sofia, she say.

But I don't have to ast Sofia. I know white people never listen to colored, period. If they do, they only listen long enough to be able to tell you what to do.

Here's the thing, say Shug. The thing I believe. God is inside you and inside everybody else. You come into the world with God. But only them that search for it inside find it. And sometimes it just manifest itself even if you not looking, or don't know what you looking for. Trouble do it for most folks, I think. Sorrow, lord. Feeling like shit.

It? I ast.

Yeah, It. God ain't a he or a she, but a It.

But what do it look like? I ast.

Don't look like nothing, she say. It ain't a picture show. It ain't something you can look at apart from anything else, including yourself. I believe God is everything, say Shug. Everything that is or ever was or ever will be. And when you can feel that, and be happy to feel that, you've found It.

Shug a beautiful something, let me tell you. She frown a little, look out cross the yard, lean back in her chair, look like a big rose.

She say, My first step from the old white man was trees. Then air. Then birds. Then other people. But one day when I was sitting quiet and feeling like a motherless child, which I was, it come to me: that feeling of being part of everything, not separate at all. I knew that if I cut a tree, my arm would bleed. And I laughed and I cried and I run all around the house. I knew just what it was. In fact, when it happen, you can't miss it. It sort of like you know what, she say, grinning and rubbing high up on my thigh.

Shug! I say.

Oh, she say. God love all them feelings. That's some of the best stuff God did. And when you know God loves 'em you enjoys 'em a lot more. You can just relax, go with everything that's going, and praise God by liking what you like.

God don't think it dirty? I ast.

Naw, she say. God made it. Listen, God love everything you love—and a mess of stuff you don't. But more than anything else, God love admiration.

You saying God vain? I ast.

Naw, she say. Not vain, just wanting to share a good thing. I think it pisses God off if you walk by the color purple in a field somewhere and don't notice it.

What it do when it pissed off? I ast.

Oh, it make something else. People think pleasing God is all God care about. But any fool living in the world can see it always trying to please us back.

Yeah? I say.

Yeah, she say. It always making little surprises and springing them on us when us least expect.

You mean it want to be loved, just like the bible say.

Yes, Celie, she say. Everything want to be loved. Us sing and dance, make faces and give flower bouquets, trying to be loved.

You ever notice that trees do everything to git attention we do, except walk?

Well, us talk and talk bout God, but I'm still adrift. Trying to chase that old white man out of my head. I been so busy thinking bout him I never truly notice nothing God make. Not a blade of corn (how it do that?) not the color purple (where it come from?). Not the little wildflowers. Nothing.

Now that my eyes opening, I feels like a fool. Next to any little scrub of a bush in my yard, Mr. —— 's evil sort of shrink. But not altogether. Still, it is like Shug say, You have to git man off your eyeball, before you can see anything a'tall.

Man corrupt everything, say Shug. He on your box of grits, in your head, and all over the radio. He try to make you think he everywhere. Soon as you think he everywhere, you think he God. But he ain't. Whenever you trying to pray, and man plop himself on the other end of it, tell him to git lost, say Shug. Conjure up flowers, wind, water, a big rock.

But this hard work, let me tell you. He been there so long, he don't want to budge. He threaten lightening, floods and earthquakes. Us fight. I hardly pray at all. Every time I conjure up a rock, I throw it.

Amen.

THE LOVE THAT IS HEREAFTER

Walt Whitman

O, BEAUTEOUS IS THE EARTH! AND FAIR
The splendors of Creation are:
Nature's green robe, the shining sky,
The winds that through the tree-tops sigh,
     All speak a bounteous God.

The noble trees, the sweet young flowers,
The birds that sing in forest bowers,
The rivers grand that murmuring roll,
And all which joys or calms the soul
     Are made by gracious might.

The flocks and droves happy and free,
The dwellers of the boundless sea,
Each living thing on air or land,
Created by our Master's hand,
     Is formed for joy and peace.

But man—weak, proud, and erring man,
Of truth ashamed, of folly vain—
Seems singled out to know no rest
And of all things that move, feels least
        The sweets of happiness.

Yet he it is whose little life
is passed in useless, vexing strife,
And all the glorious earth to him
Is rendered dull, and poor, and dim,
        From hope unsatisfied.

He faints with grief—he toils through care—
And from the cradle to the bier
He wearily plods on—till Death
Cuts short his transient, panting breath,
        And sends him to his sleep.

O, mighty powers of Destiny!
When from this coil of flesh I'm free—
When through my second life I rove,
Let me but find one heart to love,
        As I would wish to love:

Let me but meet a single breast,
Where this tired soul its hope may rest,
In never-dying faith: ah, then,
That would be bliss all free from pain,
        And sickness of the heart.

For vainly through this world below
We seek affection. Nought but woe
Is with our earthly journey wove;
And so the heart must look above,
        Or die in dull despair.

MYSTERY

Rachel Naomi Remen

I WAS LATE FOR WHAT WAS TO BE MY LAST VISIT WITH MY MOTHER. PUSHING through rush hour traffic, tired from a long day at the office, I stopped to buy her some flowers. It was seven in the evening and the florist had no purple irises, my mother's favorites, and little of anything else. Sympathizing with my distress, he offered me a bouquet of half-closed iris buds from his icebox, assuring me that they would open in a few hours. I took them and waited, irritated and impatient, as he wrapped them in green tissue. A strange-looking bouquet. Then I hurried on.

Carrying the flowers, I pushed through the heavy doors of the ward. A nurse was waiting there for me. "I'm so sorry," she said. My mother had died a short time before. Stunned, I allowed myself to be led to her room. She lay in her bed, seemingly asleep. Her hands were still warm. The nurse

… all that I know is that we are somehow alive, all of us in the light, making shadows, the sun overhead, space all around us, inhaling, exhaling, the face and form of man everywhere, pleasure and pain, sanity and madness, over and over again, war and no war, peace and no peace, the earth solid and unaware of us, unaware of our cities, our dreams, unaware of this love I have for life, the love that was the boy's, unaware of all things, my going, my coming, the earth everlastingly itself, not of me, everlastingly…

—William Saroyan

Right: Morton Livingston Schamberg, *Figure*. Schamberg's tremendous sense of color is seen in this artwork, also combined with his noted understanding of composition and form. The artist died shortly before his 37th birthday during the flu epidemic of 1918, leaving questions about what he might have been able to achieve artistically in his career.

asked if there was anyone I wanted her to call. Numbly I gave her the numbers of some of my oldest friends and sat down to wait. It was peaceful and very still in the room. One by one my friends came.

Four days later I was three thousand miles away arranging for my mother's burial. It was an unseasonably hot spring and New York City was at its worst, muggy and uncomfortable. The funeral director was a person of sensitivity and kindness. Gently he went over the arrangements, assuring himself and me again of the details of my mother's wishes which we had discussed on the phone. Then he paused. "There was something that came from California with your mother. May I show you?" he asked. Together we walked down the corridor to where my mother lay in her closed pine coffin. Lying on the coffin lid, still in the twist of green tissue paper was the bouquet I had left in my mother's hospital room on her bed. But now the irises were in full bloom. I remember them still with great clarity, each one huge and vibrant, seemingly filled with a purple sort of light. They had been out of water for four days.

It would be easy indeed to dismiss this sort of experience, not to make a simple shift in perspective or find a willingness to suspend disbelief for a moment. Not to consider adding up the column of figures in another way and wonder. The willingness to consider possibility requires a tolerance of uncertainty. I will never know whether or not I was once for a moment in the presence of my Russian grandmother or if my mother used my final gift of flowers to make me a gift of her own, letting me know that there may be more to life than the mind can understand.

Right: Cathryn Chase, *Sunken Temple.*

SKINHEAD TO GODHEAD — REDEMPTION OF A RACIST

Dan Millman

W HEN HE WAS 13, RICHARD SABINSKI attended church three times. After each visit, he would talk about God with his friends. But Richard was a troubled and angry youth. Although he spoke of God with fervor, he hated all people of other races. At 15, his churchgoing days long past, Richard started doing drugs and getting into fights and into trouble. Pushing drugs by 16, he soon had three friends selling for him. Later, he

Left: Florine Stettheimer, *Portrait of Virgil Thomson.* Stettheimer painted imaginative portraits of various artists in the 1920s and 1930s. Here the subject is the composer Virgil Thomson, who is perhaps best known for his opera *Four Saints in Three Acts.* It gives a sense of transcendent experience such as lived by the author of the story.

bought a gun and pistol-whipped a drug buyer named Terry who refused to pay him for the merchandise. He then fired several shots into the side of Terry's car.

Terry escaped and called the police, who arrested Richard, then released him when Terry declined to press charges. A few days later, Richard saw Terry riding in a truck and began tailgating him. A high-speed chase ensued in which Richard fired his gun out of his window at the fleeing car. Richard was arrested again and sentenced to eight years in prison.

The overcrowded prison, brimming with racial tension, was a war zone where hatreds were color-coded and violence was a part of everyday life. Blacks, whites, and Hispanics fought territorial wars and formed gangs for protection. Skin colors became the uniforms of opposing armies, and racism became a bond of brotherhood. Richard's hatred of nonwhites now deepened to a burning focus—his gang became a potent symbol of his identity. In prison, Richard received a criminal education that would serve him upon his release less than two years later due to overcrowded prison conditions.

Back on the streets at 19, he returned to the drug business, now with hardcore members of his prison alma mater, fellow travelers on a dark path—armed robbers, drug users, violent felons. Richard attended one satanic ritual involving drugs, wild dancing, and formal prayers to Satan.

"By the time I was 23 years old," Richard says, "I realized I was an evil person. This reflection struck me out of nowhere—I was in my backyard, suddenly overcome by great sadness about my life and what I'd become. I knelt down and asked God for mercy. It was the first time I'd prayed in 10 years. The next day, I told several friends I was going to start over and become a new person. They laughed their teeth out," he reports.

Three days later, after finishing some Chinese food at a friend's house, Richard opened his fortune cookie to find the message, "Do not leave the righteous path you have chosen."

But Richard wasn't yet ready to hear this prophetic message. That same night, he and his friends went bowling and spied six Asian men a few lanes away. Richard's profound hatred welled up inside him—any skin color other than white made him see red. He and his friends approached the Asians and started a fight. But two Black men stepped in to defend the Asians. Outnumbered, Richard and his friends left, raging about "niggers" and "gooks."

A few days later, Richard stood again in his backyard. "It was just getting dark," he said, "when I heard the sound of a bugle somewhere above me. I looked up and saw the sky split right in half. It was the eeriest thing I'd ever seen; one side of the sky was light and the other side dark. I knew without a doubt that God was asking me to change—giving me a choice. Again, I saw the darkness inside me, but this time I also saw a shaft of light, a ray of hope. I knelt down and again asked God to forgive me. All the violence, the hatred and craziness of my life flashed through my mind—all of it. I saw what a miracle it was that I had survived. I felt so grateful to be alive. I suddenly understood what a gift life is. And I knew that I wanted to do something good with mine."

Richard's vision changed his character overnight.

"The next day," he reports, "I went to the bus stop and saw a Black man waiting there alone. I looked at him and was amazed—I felt no hatred toward him. I saw he was a human being just like me. I'd never looked at a nonwhite person without that rage rising in me. Now, the rage was gone. I was so surprised. I almost started to cry. He turned toward me. I smiled and said, "Hello." It was the first kind word I had ever spoken to a man of color. Overnight, my heart had turned from stone to flesh. From that moment on, I haven't felt any racial hatred for another person."

Soon after that, Richard quit drugs, stopped fighting, and began to experience a new way of life—a brotherhood with all people. Still, he met with practical life challenges, with tests and trials. "I had to find a new way to make a living, to stabilize my life. I was poor for a while," he says.

During this period of soul-searching, Richard happened to see a Chinese man on television with fingers missing on each of his hands. The man had been tortured and persecuted for his religious activities. Deeply moved by this man's story, Richard realized that God, for reasons beyond his understanding, had given him a special compassion for the Chinese people. He resolved then and there to go to China to help the people there. Richard joined a local Chinese Christian church and was warmly embraced by his new community. He was baptized and learned to speak Mandarin. Since early 1997, Richard Sabinski has been living in and wandering through China, teaching English and telling of the miracles and grace made possible by the power of divine intervention.

Right: Evangelist Billy Graham addressing a meeting, circa 1955.

[The future] will be more human and humane. It will explore and develop the richness and capacities of the human mind and spirit. It will produce individuals who are more integrated and whole. It will be a world that prizes the individual person—the greatest of our resources. It will be a more natural world, with a renewed love and respect for nature. It will develop a more human science, based on new and less rigid concepts. Its technology will be aimed at the enhancing, rather than the exploitation, of persons and nature. It will release creativity as individuals sense their power, their capacities, their freedom.

—Carl Rogers

C A T H O L I C
D R E A M S

Richard A. Russo

I

I have a golden crucifix with a hole in its center. Bright globules of light move through my body like living creatures of mercury. I hold the cross up to my brow, where my sixth chakra would be, and center it over one of the globules. A brilliant beam of light shines out through the crucifix, illuminating all that I see... .

II

I WAS RAISED A CATHOLIC, AND DUTIFULLY ATTENDED CHURCH EACH SUNDAY UNTIL I WAS ABOUT TEN, WHEN I DEVELOPED a disturbing psychosomatic reaction. Whenever I entered a church for any reason (even a family wedding), I would begin to suffocate. After five minutes, I'd have to bolt for the door or else would pass out or vomit. After a few such episodes, my parents stopped making me go to church.

By college, I considered myself an agnostic, and thought my Catholic upbringing was behind me. I began to study Western mysticism and practice meditation. Then, in my mid-twenties, I had the following dream:

> I'm in my old church, waiting to enter a large classroom, when a stern-looking priest says he will hear my confession. I'm nervous because it's been years since I went to church and I no longer remember the ritual. I decide to say, "Father, it's been a long time since my last confession. I want to tell you my doubts about God"—but then my friend H. appears [in the dream, he resembles my father], and we begin talking about sex.

> Now I'm about eight years old. "Has the boy done something wrong?" the priest asks. "Not exactly," H. replies. "Let's say it's sort of a family matter." Some pretty girls from the Catholic school are watching. I act tough. "I didn't come to talk about sex," I yell at the priest. "There's nothing wrong with sex!"

> Now I'm an adult again, standing at the podium in the classroom continuing my lecture on sex. The audience of churchgoers is shocked. I wink at one of the girls sitting nearby and whisper, "Wait till I hit them with my arguments against the existence of God. . . ."

Thus began a vivid sequence of dreams in which my Christian upbringing again became a live issue for me. During the following months, I continued to dream of arguing with the Church authorities and disrupting services. In one fanciful dream from this period, I was a starpoint of light dancing on the lawn of the Vatican, taunting the people inside. Then, two years after the initial dream of rebellion, the issue shifted to a new level:

I'm kneeling in a huge cathedral, asking God to heal me but feeling uncertain what I believe. I want a sign. I look down at the floor and see two star patterns burned into the stone, the aftereffects of an intense light. One is yellowish, the other blue. I realize that Jesus and Mary have been here, and left these marks in the stone.

This dream had a profound impact on me. My memory of it was so vivid that it came to seem part of my waking experience. I'd been given the sign I wanted, but was not satisfied; the marks were just afterimages, not the real thing. Yet they were beautiful. I drew a picture of the two stars and kept it on my desk. I was no longer sure what I believed.

A year later, I had a very long dream in which I was part of a plot to assassinate the Pope. In the dream, I lived through most of a day, complete with detailed meetings and preparations. Finally I climbed a long flight of stairs to the top of a cathedral tower, carrying a package of poison. I was supposed to wait there for a signal from one of the other conspirators, but accidentally dropped the package. It fell to the cathedral floor just as a procession of Bishops and Cardinals was entering. The High Mass was about to begin. I rushed downstairs to retrieve the poison and ended up in the front row as the Pope began the ceremony.

I'm kneeling at the railing before the altar. I look up at the altar and see a large crucifix there. I realize it's life-sized, then, to my astonishment, that a living person is hanging there. It's Christ Himself! The Pope is saying that we are all "in the service of Christ," whereupon Jesus blesses the congregation, then turns to me, smiles and says, "Even you, Russo." Suddenly, I know in my heart that it's true, and that I could never carry out my part in the assassination plot. . . .

A few months later, I had a lovely dream in which I stepped outside to receive a "blessing." It was raining, and I realized that that was the blessing, for I was being splashed with "little drops of holy water." Then, almost exactly five years after it began, the long sequence of Catholic dreams came to an end. I was in a church very much like the one in my first dream. My son and his friends were there, but the priest was late. I was going to have to fill in for him. At first I was nervous, then I began to sing a hymn, and the congregation joined me and I realized it wasn't going to be so hard after all.

III

For several years I had no more overt Christian dreams. Then, on February 13, 1978, I had two profound dreams during the same night.

In the first dream, I was in the bedroom of my childhood home. I asked my mother who the three priests in our living room were, and she replied, "That's Father Bramman . . . they're all Brammans." When I walked into the living room, no one was there. Father Bramman was waiting for me in the kitchen. I had to go through the Purification alone.

I'm kneeling, holding a candle whose flame has gone out. As I concentrate on it, two lighted candles appear, hovering in the air to form a triangle with mine. The three small candles merge to form one. Then I have a vision of an even greater and brighter candle, burning in mid-air before me.

[In one version of the dream, the flame jumps from the smaller candles to mine; in another, the three candles merge; in yet another, the greater, incorporeal flame lights my candle, then the three become one. It was all of these, and none; I cannot explain it].

My candle is lighted. As it burns gently in my hand, I hear music coming from the next room: a gospel song about "The Greater Love." [The music slowly grows louder, matching my swelling emotions, until it permeates the dream]. *My little candle begins to connect to the incorporeal one beyond. I start sobbing. The music swells, I can't stop crying. A voice says, "Isn't it time you stopped resisting? You were here once before, and didn't go on—isn't it because you were afraid of failing?" I'm crying uncontrollably as my little candle merges with the Greater One. Father Bramman peers out from the kitchen. Tears and mucous are streaming down my face, but I can't stop crying. Energy is being released all over my body. It feels so good. . . .*

I awoke from this dream around three in the morning, still trembling from my sobbing. My body was limp. I wrote down my experience, then went back to sleep.

Three black-robed, hooded monks enter the field next to our house. I am frightened and step out into the front yard to investigate, but one of them holds up his hand to indicate that I should come no closer. What is about to happen is not for me.

The three figures kneel in the field. The tall one in the middle pulls back his hood. It's Max Von Sydow! [who played the Knight in Bergman's film, "The Seventh Seal"]. He gazes upward. Dark clouds are gathering in the sky. A storm is brewing. Suddenly the clouds part and a beam of celestial light shines down on his face. A voice is saying, "It was Laughter, it was Holy God." He floats off the ground, still kneeling, and slowly ascends the beam of light, leaving the others behind in the field. As he passes through the opening into the heavens, the clouds close behind him and he disappears from view. . . .

I awoke feeling shaken and humbled by what I had lived through that night, and could not go back to sleep. The three monks entering our field had frightened me because I sensed that their presence meant Death—yet almost immediately I'd been given a signal that the dream was not about me in any literal way, that I shouldn't be afraid I was going to die. The arrival of three priests (a central "Father" figure flanked by two assistants) and the theme of merging with a "Greater Light" clearly linked the two dreams, and in the days that followed, I thought of them as a unit. My body felt shaken and empty from the deep sobbing. I felt that I'd reached a turning point in my life, heralded by the first dream. The second dream seemed to be a gloss on the first, primarily to insure that I didn't mistake the transformation I was going through for a physical process (my death).

As the days passed, I gradually came down from the intense energy of the dream, and felt a little sad that life was returning to normal. Then, about three weeks later, my sister called long distance to tell me that my father was in the hospital and had been diagnosed as having cancer. I was stunned. I hung up and started crying. I *knew* he was going to die. Later, when I had calmed a little, I realized how I knew: I'd been shown what was going to happen in my dream. The hooded monk who'd gestured to me had been right; my role was to serve as witness.

IV

My father died four months later. His illness brought me closer to my family and intensified the feelings and confusion which had been raised by my dreams. It would take more than a year to live through and resolve those issues and feelings in my waking life, yet everything, from my father's death and my grief to the need to reexamine my life, had been given to me in that one night of dreaming.

During the four months of his illness, crucifixes began appearing in my dreams. In one, I drove Satan away by holding up a cross; in another, I held a crucifix over my brow chakra and golden beams of light shone forth. (I loved that image with its double meaning: I *saw* through the crucifix, which illuminated everything before me, and I "saw through" it, the way one would see through a ruse.)

My earliest relationship to the Numinous had been through Catholicism. Now, in a time of personal crisis, my dreams had seized that channel to forge the connection anew. The important thing was the connection, the reawakening of the spiritual dimension of my life. I no longer needed to *believe* or *deny*. I could simply accept with grace whatever experience was given to me.

V

I continued to dream of my father for many months after he died. In some dreams he was telling me things. In many of them he was leaving or getting ready to leave—to slip away from his hospital room, to move out of our old house, to journey aboard a UFO.

Then, one last dream. It reminded me of another dream I once had in which Time had stopped, and I had to go to the basement of a great library to write the name of each book in golden letters on its spine. As I did my work, the books came alive, until finally Time started moving forward again.

This dream seemed to be the reverse of that earlier one. I felt detached from it, like it was someone else's dream, even though I experienced it as my own. When I woke from it, I immediately thought of my father.

Perhaps it was his dream.

Someone gives me a book as a gift. It's a hardcover copy of Ragtime. *I put some glue on it to bind it, but instead the binding starts to dissolve. The glue had sulphuric acid in it! As I watch, the binding continues to soften, then the words begin to fade away, until finally the whole book is blank. . . .*

. . . Now the world is dissolving. I'm afraid that death will mean the end of me. Details keep fading away until finally there's nothing left. I'm in a reddish void. But I am. The point of consciousness that is me endures. . . .

Left: Sarah Pletts, *Target*. Although seen by the subject of the poem, the face of God is traditionally unseeable and unknowable. In order to depict the unknowable divinity, the simple perfection of the circle is often used by different religious traditions.

FATHER MAPPLE'S HYMN

Herman Melville

THE RIBS AND TERRORS IN THE WHALE
Arched over me a dismal gloom,
While all God's sun-lit waves rolled by,
And lift me deepening down to doom.

I saw the opening maw of hell,
With endless pains and sorrows there;
Which none but they that feel can tell—
Oh, I was plunging to despair.

In black distress, I called my God,
When I could scarce believe him mine,
He bowed his ear to my complaints—
No more the whale did me confine.

With speed he flew to my relief,
As on a radiant dolphin borne;
Awful, yet bright, as lightning shone
The face of my Deliverer God.

My song for ever shall record
That terrible, that joyful hour;
I give the glory to my God,
His all the mercy and the power.

FOREVER YOUNG

Ronald Steel

Fit and well-tanned trendoes flocked to idylls such as Jackson Hole, Aspen, Santa Fe, and Tahoe in the eighties, searching for purity and authenticity, blissing out, getting in touch with nature. Hollywood arrived and these resorts became even more showy. But keeping up with cool demanded a lot of cash and God forbid that one might smoke a cigarette or be twenty pounds overweight.

WE SWOOPED IN LOW THROUGH AMAZING PEAKS AND DROPPED DOWN INTO A LUSH VALLEY DOTTED WITH condos as far as the eye could see. I had a café crème and pain au chocolat at the airport snack bar, and watched the suntans and tennis rackets come and go. Eventually I sauntered over to an exceedingly hip clerk and asked when he thought my bags might be in. "No problem," he reassured me. "On the next plane from Denver. Or maybe the one after. They always come through eventually." No hurry. No problem.

Donning my cool, I hopped into a Mellow Yellow taxi and headed for the village of Aspen, which nestles in a valley cupped between mountains as lushly green as Astroturf. Between the simulated redwood and cedar condos are sprinkled quaint Victorian houses in hues of apricot, fuchsia, and heather, San Francisco style. They and their quarter-acre plots sell for upward of $400,000 each. Only a commodity trader or a cocaine dealer could afford them. Happily Aspen has many such entrepreneurs. Most, however, prefer to live on the slopes of the mountain overlooking the town. There they build multiterraced dwellings with huge sheets of glass

Right: Dancing hippies at a pop festival in 1970. The materialistic Cult of Youth in this story is a strange consequence of the hippy movement with its rejection of the values of the previous generations.

wrapped around jutting timbers. From marbled Jacuzzis they watch the last rays of the sun bathe Aspen Mountain in a golden Krugerrand glow and ponder the justice of a system that has brought them such rewards.

Not everyone in Aspen is rich, or even young, though a first-time visitor would be apt to think so. All the men seem to be 32 years old with sandy mustaches, bulging pectorals, and perpetual tans. All the women are 29, with straight blond hair, fashionably flat chests, and long legs. (For summer tourists subtract ten years.) Naturally none of these people was born here. All come from Cedar Rapids, Bayonne, or Dayton. Most of them work at one thing or another, though the jobs are usually below both their level of education and expectation. They are waitresses and tour guides and carpenters and clerks. They are here not to advance themselves—there is nowhere much to go, except in the real estate business—but simply to prolong the Aspen experience. You can see them jogging along the streets and bicycle trails, even up the mountain roads. They breathe easily, despite the thinness of the air at 8,000 feet. Their smooth complexions are rarely marred by a drop of sweat.

Keeping in shape is a tyranny from which there is no respite. But for the golden young people of Aspen it is the affirmation of the good life. It is also the passport into it, for fatties are not permitted. And a good life it is: congenial folks, amusing restaurants, a constant inflow of new bodies, and hardly a rumble of the troubles that preoccupy the outside world. The very rich fly in and out on their Lear jets to check up on their property and test the slopes or the tennis courts. The locals house-sit for them and provide services that the rich require. This allows the youngish locals to stay on in their Shangri-La. Few of them can afford to live in Aspen itself. The tourists and second-home fatcats have driven property values up so high that those who actually do the work in Aspen have been mostly forced to live in cheaper locales down the road. They drive in every day as commuters to the town that was taken away from them.

They come for the scenery, which is as spectacular as it's supposed to be; for the hassle-free existence, which they can have, within certain sharp limits; for the days that are interchangeable in their bucolic ordinariness, and the nights that offer hope of instant adventure or psychic transformation; for the anticipation of the first run down the slopes on last night's powder snow; for the experience of living on a *Zauberberg* just a little bit outside of time; for the possibility that tomorrow a beautiful (or rich) stranger will walk into their lives and all will be changed magically. The place lends itself to dreams. Not so long ago it was a scruffy mining town that time and venture capitalists had forgotten.

Others had come here once before in search of instant riches, built their palaces, spent their money, and then went off to hitch their broken dreams to other stars. Down the road a piece of Aspen, tucked away in the folds of a valley green in summer but totally snowbound in winter, lie the remnants of a little village called Ashworth. It was once as rich and sinful as Babel, or even Aspen. Chanteuses came to sing from Europe; gamblers and whores would snatch up your money in a glorious flash you'd remember for a lifetime. Now it's a few weathered boards, the wind whistling through the cracks, and a faint echo of coyotes. *Sic transit.* But that isn't the lesson of Aspen either. All dreams speed by too fast, all Xanadus become cracked boards and dust. When was it any different? So why not dance a little faster under the strobe light at the Paragon Café–the one in front of the video camera that captures your image and projects it on a screen above you, so that you can see yourself on MTV? To be the observer of oneself—what could be more tantalizing or forbiddingly satisfying? Who can even bother to notice one's partner at such an epiphanic moment? Come back tomorrow night for more.

Does the image ever fade? Does the time ever come when you say: I don't want to watch myself being watched? I don't care if I get fat? I get tired of being cool? I'm choking on fresh air, whole grain biscuits, and raw milk? I want to ride the subway? The answer is: I don't know. I didn't stay long enough. I walked through fields of asphodels so high up in the peaks called the Maroon Bells that I thought I could hear them ringing. A few hours later I lounged in a hot tub watching a double rainbow that appeared after a spectacular lightning storm that left half the sky purple-black and the other half baby-blue dotted with raspberry-lemon clouds. Why be upwardly mobile? I asked myself. Is there anything up there at the top of the ladder? Why not kiss the A Train and the Sheridan Road Express and the Harbor Freeway goodbye? Why not just take another hike into a wilderness of crater lakes and mountain meadows? Maybe I'd stayed on too long myself. Or not long enough. I ordered another Margarita and decided to think about it tomorrow.

MAKING YOUR LIFE MEANINGFUL

The Dalai Lama

W HEN I MEET PEOPLE IN DIFFERENT parts of the world, I am always reminded that we are all basically alike: we are all human beings. Maybe we wear different clothes, our skin is of a different color, or we speak different languages. These are only superficial differences, basically, we are the same human beings. That is what makes it possible for us to understand each other and to develop friendship and closeness.

Here let me share with you a short prayer which gives me great inspiration in my own quest to be of benefit to others:

May I become at all times, both now and forever
A protector for those without protection
A guide for those who have lost their way
A ship for those with oceans to cross
A bridge for those with rivers to cross
A sanctuary for those in danger
A lamp for those without light
A place of refuge for those who lack shelter
And a servant to all in need.

The core of this advice is to make your life as meaningful as possible. There is nothing mysterious about it. It consists in nothing more than acting out of concern for others. And provided you undertake this practice sincerely and with persistence, you will gradually be able to reorder your habits and attitudes so that you think less about your own narrow concerns and more of others'. In doing so, you will find that you enjoy peace and happiness yourself.

Relinquish your envy, let go your desire to triumph over others. Instead, try to benefit them. With kindness, with courage, and confident that in doing so you are sure to meet with success, welcome others with a smile. Be straightforward. And try to be impartial. Treat everyone as if they were a close friend. I say this as a human being: one who, like yourself, wishes to be happy and not miserable.

If you cannot, for whatever reason, be of help to others, at least don't harm them. Consider yourself a tourist. Think of the world

Left: Sarah Pletts, *Glitter Buddha.*

as it is seen from space, so small and insignificant yet so beautiful. Could there really be anything to be gained from harming others during our stay here? Is it not preferable, and more reasonable, to relax and enjoy ourselves quietly, just as if we were visiting a different neighborhood? Therefore, if in the midst of your enjoyment of the world you have a moment, try to help in however small a way those who are downtrodden and those who, for whatever reason, cannot or do not help themselves. Try not to turn away from those whose appearance is disturbing, from the ragged and unwell. Try never to think of them as inferior to yourself. If you can, try not even to think of yourself as better than the humblest beggar, for we will all look the same in the grave.

Because we all share this small planet earth, we have to learn to live in harmony and peace with each other and with nature. That is not just a dream but a necessity. We are dependent on each other in so many ways that we can no longer live in isolated communities and ignore what is happening outside those communities. We need to help each other when we have difficulties, and we must share the good fortune that we enjoy.

I would also like to mention here the plight and aspirations of the people of Tibet. As a free spokesman for my fellow country men and women, I feel it is my duty to speak out on their behalf. But I do so not with a feeling of anger or hatred toward those who are responsible for the immense suffering of our people and the destruction of our land, homes, and culture. I make a distinction between the action and its perpetrator. Moreover the Chinese too are human beings who struggle to find happiness and deserve our compassion. I do so simply to draw attention to the sad situation in my country today and to the aspirations of my people, because in our struggle for freedom, truth is the only weapon we possess.

We Tibetans also hope to contribute to the development of a more peaceful, more humane, and more beautiful world. A future free Tibet

"Meaningless! Meaningless! says the Teacher.
"Utterly meaningless! Everything is meaningless."
What does man gain from all his labor at which he toils under the sun?
Generations come and generations go, but the earth remains forever.
The sun rises and the sun sets, and hurries back to where it rises.
The wind blows to the south and turns to the north; round and round it goes, ever turning on its course.
All streams flow into the sea, yet the sea is never full.
To the place the streams come from, there they return again.

—Ecclesiastes 1:13

will seek to help those in need throughout the world, to protect nature, and to promote peace. I believe that the Tibetan ability to combine spiritual qualities with a realistic and practical attitude can enable us to make a special contribution in however modest a way.

Finally, let me conclude with another verse from the great eighth century Indian Buddhist master, Shantideva:

> For as long as space endures,
> And for as long as living beings remain,
> Until then may I, too, abide
> To dispel the misery of the world.

TELL ME NOT, IN MOURNFUL NUMBERS,
"Life is but an empty dream!"
For the soul is dead that slumbers,
And things are not what they seem.

Life is real! Life is earnest!
And the grave is not its goal;
"Dust thou art, to dust returnest,"
Was not spoken of the soul.

Not enjoyment, and not sorrow,
Is our destined end or way;
But to act, that each tomorrow
Finds us farther than today.

Left: Neil Armstrong, *Buzz Aldrin on the Moon.* The photograph of Edwin E. ('Buzz') Aldrin, one of the first men on the moon, taken on July 20, 1969, is one of the 20th century's most resonant images. The poem's call to heroic acts and to "leave behind us footprints on the sands of time" is certainly evoked by this image.

A PSALM OF LIFE

Henry Wadsworth Longfellow

(What the heart of the young man said to the psalmist)

Art is long, and Time is fleeting,
And our hearts, though stout and brave,
Still, like muffled drums, are beating
Funeral marches to the grave.

In the world's broad field of battle,
In the bivouac of Life,
Be not like dumb, driven cattle!
Be a hero in the strife!

Trust no Future, howe'er pleasant!
Let the dead Past bury its dead!
Act, act in the living Present!
Heart within, and God o'erhead!

Lives of great men all remind us
We can make our lives sublime,
And, departing, leave behind us
Footprints on the sands of time;

Footprints, that perhaps another,
Sailing o'er life's solemn main,
A forlorn and shipwrecked brother,
Seeing, shall take heart again.

Let us, then, be up and doing,
With a heart for any fate;
Still achieving, still pursuing,
Learn to labour and to wait.

FREE AT LAST

Martin Luther King

Now is the time to make real the promise of democracy.

Now is the time to rise from the dark and desolate valley of segregation to the sunlit path of racial justice.

Now is the time to lift our nation from the quicksands of racial injustice to the solid rock of brotherhood.

Now is the time to make justice a reality to all of God's children. . . .

Right: Dr. Martin Luther King, Jr., civil rights activist, addresses a large crowd at the Lincoln Memorial for the March on Washington, Washington, DC, August 28, 1963.

I still have a dream. It is a dream deeply rooted in the American dream.

I have a dream that one day this nation will rise up and live out the true meaning of its creed. We hold these truths to be self-evident that all men are created equal.

I have a dream that one day out in the red hills of Georgia the sons of former slaves and the sons of former slave owners will be able to sit down together at the table of brotherhood.

I have a dream that one day even the state of Mississippi, a state sweltering with the heat of oppression, will be transformed into an oasis of freedom and justice.

I have a dream that my four little children will one day live in a nation where they will not be judged by the color of their skin but by their character.

I have a dream today.

I have a dream that one day down in Alabama, with its vicious racists, with its governor having his lips dripping with the words of interposition and nullification; that one day right down in Alabama little black boys and black girls will be able to join hands with little white boys and white girls as sisters and brothers.

I have a dream today.

I have a dream that one day every valley shall be engulfed, every hill shall be exalted and every mountain shall be made low, the rough places will be made plains and the crooked places will be

Our struggle is not easy. Those who oppose our cause are rich and powerful and they have many allies in high places. We are poor. Our allies are few. But we have something the rich do not own. We have our own bodies and spirits and the justice of our cause as our weapons. When we are really honest with ourselves we must admit that our lives are all that really belong to us. So, it is how we use our lives that determines what kind of men we are. It is my deepest belief that only by giving our lives do we find life. I am convinced that the truest act of courage, the strongest act of manliness is to sacrifice ourselves for others in a totally non-violent struggle for justice. To be a man is to suffer for others. God help us to be men!

—Cesar Chavez, 1968

made straight and the glory of the Lord shall be revealed and all flesh shall see it together.

This is our hope. This is the faith that I will go back to the South with. With this faith we will be able to hew out of the mountain of despair a stone of hope.

With this faith we will be able to transform the jangling discords of our nation into a beautiful symphony of brotherhood.

With this faith we will be able to work together, to pray together, to struggle together, to go to jail together, to climb up for freedom together, knowing that we will be free one day. '

This will be the day when all of God's children will be able to sing with new meaning "My country 'tis of thee, sweet land of liberty, of thee I sing. Land where my fathers died, land of the Pilgrim's pride, from every mountainside, let freedom ring!"

And if America is to be a great nation, this must become true. So let freedom ring from the hilltops of New Hampshire. Let freedom ring from the mighty mountains of New York.

Let freedom ring from the heightening Alleghenies of Pennsylvania.

Let freedom ring from the snow-capped Rockies of Colorado.

Let freedom ring from the curvaceous slopes of California.

But not only that, let freedom, ring from Stone Mountain of Georgia.

Let freedom ring from every hill and molehill of Mississippi and every mountainside.

When we let freedom ring, when we let it ring from every tenement and every hamlet, from every state and every city, we will be able to speed up that day when all of God's children, black men and white men, Jews and Gentiles, Protestants and Catholics, will be able to join hands and sing in the words of the old spiritual, "Free at last, free at last. Thank God Almighty, we are free at last."

T H E   S O U L   O F   A N   I N D I A N

Charles Eastman (Ohiyesa), 1911

THE ORIGINAL ATTITUDE OF THE AMERICAN INDIAN TOWARD THE ETERNAL, THE "GREAT MYSTERY" THAT SURROUNDS and embraces us, was as simple as it was exalted. To him it was the supreme conception, bringing with it the fullest measure of joy and satisfaction possible in this life.

The worship of the "Great Mystery" was silent, solitary, free from all self-seeking. It was silent, because all speech is of necessity feeble and imperfect; therefore the souls of my ancestors ascended to God in wordless adoration. It was solitary, because they believed that He is nearer to us in solitude, and there were no priests authorized to come between a man and his Maker. None might exhort or confess or in any way meddle with the religious experience of another. Among us all men were created sons of God and stood erect, as conscious of their divinity. Our faith might not be formulated in creeds, nor forced upon any who were unwilling to receive it; hence there was no preaching, proselytizing, nor persecution, neither were there any scoffers or atheists.

There were no temples or shrines among us save those of nature. Being a natural man, the Indian was intensely poetical. He would deem it sacrilege to build a house for Him who may be met face to face in the mysterious, shadowy aisles of the primeval forest, or on the sunlit bosom of virgin prairies, upon dizzy spires and pinnacles of naked rock, and yonder in the jeweled vault of the night sky! He who enrobes Himself in filmy veils

Right: David F. Barry, *Sitting Bull, or Tata'nka I'Yota'nka* [*The great Sioux Medicine Man, killed by U.S. Indian Police, December 18, 1890*]

of cloud, there on the rim of the visible world where our Great-Grandfather Sun kindles his evening camp-fire, He who rides upon the rigorous wind of the north, or breathes forth His spirit upon aromatic southern airs, whose war—canoe is launched upon majestic rivers and inland seas—He needs no lesser cathedral!

That solitary communion with the Unseen which was the highest expression of our religious life is partly described in the word *bambeday*, literally "mysterious feeling," which has been variously translated "fasting" and "dreaming." It may better be interpreted as "consciousness of the divine."

The foundations of a person are not in matter but in spirit.

—Ralph Waldo Emerson

HOMELESS

Doris Colmes

I'M CAREENING DOWN THE BACK ALLEY to my house, when suddenly I'm forced to slam on the brakes. There, propped up against the fence, his legs stretched out directly onto the tire-tracks is a homeless person of the large furry variety. You know. Full curly beard, hat with hair peeking out from under the earflaps, parka a bit too tight, pants a bit too short, shopping cart nearby. There he sits, a bottle of Thunderbird carefully perched on his lap, staring at nothing in the chill March drizzle. And his legs prevent the car from reaching its destination. I lean out the window.

"Hey, move your legs."

No response.

"Hey man, move your legs."

Aroused from his inner visions, he looks up.

"I'm from Minnesota."

"Well, cool, but you gotta move your legs."

"I'm cold."

"Hey, you're from Minnesota. Minnesota is cold."

"Yeah, but it's a different kind. This here is damp, chill, wet cold. This is colder."

"Well, OK, but you gotta move your legs."

"I was in treatment in Minnesota for eight months, but it didn't take, so I came here."

"You still have to move your legs, though."

"Move my legs?"

"Yeah, I can't get to the garage till you move your legs."

"I don't think I can get up."

I jump out and get him turned to the side, so he can get an assist form the fence and then squat, get my shoulder under his armpit and heave. Somehow, in concerted effort, we get him erect. Kind of. I take a good look and say, "OK, now wait till I get the car in the garage. OK?" No reply. He is back gazing at whatever he sees in the gray distance.

In the garage, I open my wallet. I know for a fact that there is a ten dollar bill in there, nestling amongst the singles. And then I, notorious skinflint, champion of the world's penurious, consistent winner of the monthly battle between my teensy little social security income versus the cost of living, I go for that ten.

There he still teeters, propped into a standing position by the fence, still looking into space.

"Hey, listen. Here's ten bucks. Now, what you gotta do is get yourself down the street to that

Left: Andrew Lane, *Untitled.* A homeless man on the steps of a church in New York.

MacDonald's and get in there, you hear? Get in there and sit and order something hot to eat. You got that? Go to the MacDonald's down the street, get in there, order something hot to eat and then just sit. OK?"

He looks at the money, looks at me, his eyes big and shining. He does not take the money. I reach for his hand, remove its fingerless glove, put the money in his palm and then wrestle the glove back on.

"Now: Get to the MacDonald's, go inside, order something hot and sit. OK?" His eyes widen in surprise. He comes out of his trance. From his vantage point of giant furriness, he looks down at me—the little old retired lady—smiles and asks, "Can I have a hug?"

"You betcha."

I disappear into his huge enfoldment and smile up at his face.

"You remind me of my mother. You have eyes like my mother. My mother died when she was fifty-three. She was an alcoholic."

"Wow, that's tough. Sometimes alcoholism comes down through the genes. Makes recovery hard, doesn't it."

Arm in arm, we walk through the fence gate towards my back door. We look into each other's eyes like two old friends about to part forever.

"Are you an alcoholic?"

"Addict. In Recovery. Now, remember, go to the MacDonald's, order something hot and just sit. OK?"

"OK."

We touch one another's shoulders and then he bumbles back out the gate to retrieve his Thunderbird and shopping cart. After a while, I hear the cart rattling off in the distance, towards the MacDonald's.

Now, six months later, everything's the same and everything's different. Life lurches on as usual. The dog is still senile and confused about

Since the stars have fallen from heaven and our highest symbols have paled, a secret life holds sway in the unconscious. . . . Our unconscious, on the other hand, hides living water, spirit that has become nature, and that is why it is disturbed. Heaven has become for us the cosmic space of the physicists, and the divine empyrean a fair memory of things that once were. But "the heart glows," and a secret unrest gnaws at the roots of our being.

—Carl Gustav Jung

everything except food and my own short-term memory just about matches his. The social security check is still teensy, the weeds continue winning their relentless war against what's left of the lawn and my knee still hurts after jogging.

But, inside of me, at the very core, there is a steady light. It stays on, no matter what else is happening, warm and comforting. And I think of him every day: My guardian angel, that divine messenger who bestowed upon me a gift directly from God.

In our few moments, God, using "Mr. Minnesota" as His delivery person, returned to me a part of myself I hadn't even known was missing. A last little misplaced piece of my soul, tiny but vital. And the gift continues to grow. Each day it brings new serenity. and I, without even understanding its full meaning, somehow share it.

I thank God, daily, for the gift and for His divine messenger. I know that somewhere, somehow, "Mr. Minnesota" is asking for a hug from someone and giving back exactly whatever blessing he recipient needs. Isn't it wonderful how those messengers come? Disguised in clown suits, or grubby jeans, in fancy ballgowns or as furry homeless alcoholics, there they are, just waiting for us to open our hearts so the gifts can enter.

Baruch Bashan: The blessings already are.

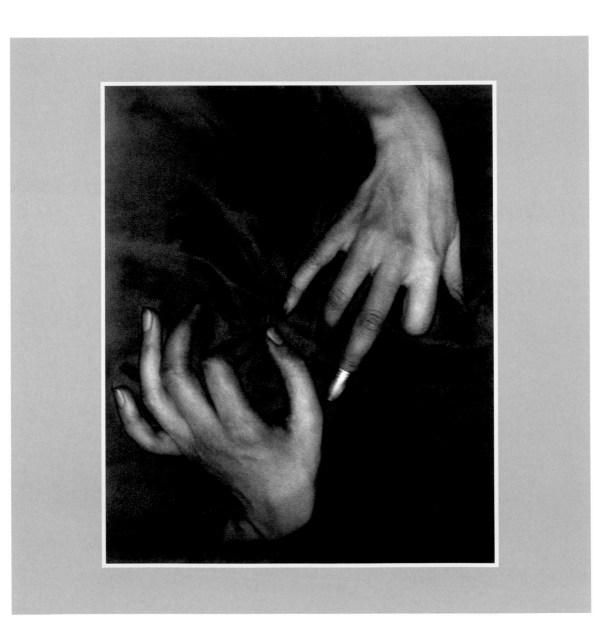

MEETING HELEN KELLER

Jean Houston

SOMETIMES I FEEL SIGHTLESS AND SENSELESS. SOMETIMES—TOO OFTEN IF THE TRUTH be told—I look out through the hazy portholes of my mind's body and detect only occasional glimmerings of who or what is out there. I yearn to know, and I know that my yearning is not enough. The world is mute, and time seems a vast conspiracy of silence. I look inward, and the inhabitants of that arcane and beautiful country flash by like shy comets. Who are they, I wonder, and who or what is their place in the order of things? And who or what are you sitting there reading my musings? Do you muse in like manner, I wonder? Are we together a museum of lonely musing pieces stammering our frustration on the edge of eternity? What key is needed to unlock the coding; what hand tapping the alphabet of creation into our outstretched palms is near to awakening that all-but-forgotten memory of who we are, and what it's all about?

I met Helen Keller once. I went to one of the great public schools of the world, P.S. 6 in New York. Our teachers, some of whom had been taught by

Left: Alfred Stieglitz, *Georgia O'Keeffe* Helen Keller's hands were one of her only ways of communication with the world and her touch "lifted into radiance" the young girl in this piece.   **Right Top:** Barry Peterson, *Hands - Variation 2.*   **Right Bottom:** Barry Peterson, *Hands - Variation 3.*

John Dewey, were offering to special classes experimental programs in multi-modal education. We learned mathematics by dancing, studied the Native Americans by preparing and eating Indian foods and building teepees, and, most important, we were taken to meet the great elders of the times. I was about eight or nine when I was taken across the river to meet Albert Einstein, who I remember as being extremely vague and as having a great head of hair.

That same year our teacher, Miss O'Reilly, took us to meet Helen Keller. Before we got on the bus to go somewhere in the East 60's, she read us the powerful passage in which Helen Keller writes that for the first six years of her life, she had no concepts whatsoever; her mind was muddy and closed off. Finally her teacher, Annie Sullivan, in a fit of frustration, pulled her out to the ivy-covered well house, pumped a cool, clear something into one of her hands, while she spelled W-A-T-E-R over and over again into the other.

> . . . I stood still, my whole attention fixed upon the motions of her fingers. Suddenly I felt a misty consciousness as of something forgotten—a thrill of returning thought; and somehow the mystery of language was revealed to me. I knew then that "w-a-t-e-r" meant the wonderful cool something that was flowing over my hand. That living word awakened my soul, gave it light, hope, joy, set it free! There were barriers still, it is true, but barriers that could in time be swept away.

As Miss O'Reilly continued to read to us from Miss Keller's autobiography, I too could feel sweet strange things begin to wing themselves over my mind. It was almost, but not quite, like an awakening to what I had long forgotten. With Helen however, the awakening was complete. The word *water* dropped into her mind like the sun into a frozen, winter world, and she learned the names for thirty things before the end of that day.

With this preparation, Class 4B got on the bus. Miss Keller was radiant, utterly radiant! I had never seen anybody in my entire life so full of joy. To be in the same room with her was to be in a space so filled with presence it was like being exposed to an electrical charge. She must have been sixty-eight or sixty-nine at the time—very beautiful, a big woman, about five foot eight or so. She spoke to us in an awesome voice, which has been described as the voice of a pythoness, an oracle. She had never heard speech since the age of nineteen months, so her inflections were all over the place.

I remember being so deeply moved that I knew I had to speak to her. I didn't know what I wanted to say, I just knew that I had to speak to her. When we were asked if there were any questions, I raised my hand. Normally the companion who was with her—it was Polly Thomson—would tap out the questions for her, but children who wanted to talk more directly to her were allowed to go up to Miss Keller to ask their question. I remember that she reached out to me and put her entire hand over my face. It seems to me now that the center of her palm was on my lips; the rest of her hand and fingers were reading my face and expression. Still I didn't know what to say, so I just blurted out what was in my heart, "Why are you so happy?"

She laughed, and laughed, and laughed, and then she said in that awesome voice of hers, "My child, it is because I live each day as if it were my last, and life in all its moments is so full of glory."

Her hands lingered on my face for a moment, and again I felt as if I were lifted into radiance, and some kind of a charge passed between us. I was never again quite the same, and I will never forget her. She was certainly in my experience the most illumined human being I ever met. Despite living in a world of utter darkness and no sound, she operated on many, many more levels and with many, many more senses than anyone else I have ever known.

THE   BRIDGE

Edwin Friedman

THERE WAS A MAN WHO HAD GIVEN MUCH THOUGHT TO WHAT HE wanted from life. He had experienced many moods and trials. He had experimented with different ways of living, and he had had his share of both success and failure. At last, he began to see clearly where he wanted to go.

Diligently, he searched for the right opportunity. Sometimes he came close, only to be pushed away. Often he applied all his strength and imagination. only to find the path hopelessly blocked. And then at last it came. But the opportunity would not wait. It would be made available only for a short time. If it were seen that he was not committed, the opportunity would not come again.

Eager to arrive, he started on his journey. With each step, he wanted to move faster; with each thought about his goal, his heart beat quicker; with each vision of what lay ahead, he found renewed

Right: Sarah Pletts, *Peace Shrine*. In this shrine, symbols of different religions exist in harmony and create depth and richness, just as the man in this story had lived a full life exploring many different paths.

vigor. Strength that had left him since his early youth returned, and desires, all kinds of desires, reawakened from their long-dormant positions.

Hurrying along, he came upon a bridge that crossed through the middle of a town. It had been built high above a river in order to protect it from the floods of spring.

He started across. Then he noticed someone coming from the opposite direction. As they moved closer, it seemed as though the other were coming to greet him. He could see clearly, however, that he did not know this other, who was dressed similarly except for something tied around his waist.

When they were within hailing distance, he could see that what the other had about his waist was a rope. It was wrapped around him many times and probably, if extended, would reach a length of 30 feet.

The other began to uncurl the rope, and, just as they were coming close, the stranger said, "Pardon me, would you be so kind as to hold the end a moment?"

Surprised by this politely phrased but curious request, he agreed without a thought, reached out, and took it.

"Thank you," said the other, who then added, "two hands now, and remember, hold tight." Whereupon, the other jumped off the bridge.

Quickly, the free-falling body hurtled the distance of the rope's length, and from the bridge the man abruptly felt the pull. Instinctively, he held tight and was almost dragged over the side. He managed to brace himself against the edge, however, and after having caught his breath, looked down at the other dangling, close to oblivion.

"What are you trying to do?" he yelled.

"Just hold tight," said the other.

"This is ridiculous," the man thought and began trying to haul the other in. He could not get the leverage, however. It was as though the weight of the other person and the length of the rope had been carefully calculated in advance so that together they created a counterweight just beyond his strength to bring the other back to safety.

"Why did you do this?" the man called out.

"Remember," said the other, "if you let go, I will be lost."

"But I cannot pull you up," the man cried.

"I am your responsibility," said the other.

"Well, I did not ask for it," the man said.

"If you let go, I am lost," repeated the other.

He began to look around for help. But there was no one. How long would he have to wait? Why did this happen to befall him now, just as he was on the verge of true success? He examined the side, searching for a place to tie the rope. Some protrusion, perhaps, or maybe a hole in the boards. But the railing was unusually uniform in shape; there were no spaces between the boards. There was no way to get rid of this newfound burden, even temporarily.

"What do you want?" he asked the other hanging below.

"Just your help," the other answered.

"How can I help? I cannot pull you in, and there is no place to tie the rope so that I can go and find someone to help me help you."

"I know that. Just hang on; that will be enough. Tie the rope around your waist; it will be easier."

Fearing that his arms could not hold out much longer, he tied the rope around his waist.

"Why did you do this?" he asked again. "Don't you see what you have done? What possible purpose could you have had in mind?"

"Just remember," said the other, "my life is in your hands. "

What should he do? "If I let go, all my life I will know that I let this other die. If I stay, I risk losing my momentum toward my own long-sought-after salvation. Either way this will haunt me forever." With ironic humor he thought to die himself, instantly, to jump off the bridge while still holding on. "That would teach this fool." But he wanted to live and to live life fully. "What a choice I have to make; how shall I ever decide?"

As time went by, still no one came. The critical moment of decision was drawing near. To show his commitment to his own goals, he would have to continue on his journey now. It was already almost. too late to arrive in time. But what a terrible choice to have to make.

A new thought occurred to him. While he could not pull this other up solely by his own efforts, if the other would shorten the rope from his end by curling it around his waist again and again, together they could do it. Actually, the other could do it by himself, so long as he, standing on the bridge, kept it still and steady.

"Now listen," he shouted down. "I think I know how to save you." And he explained his plan.

But the other wasn't interested.

"You mean you won't help? But I told you I cannot pull you up myself, and I don't think I can hang on much longer either."

"You must try," the other shouted back in tears. "If you fail, I die."

The point of decision arrived. What should he do? "My life or this other's?" And then a new idea. A revelation. So new, in fact, it seemed heretical, so alien was it to his traditional way of thinking.

"I want you to listen carefully," he said, "because I mean what I am about to say. I will not accept the position of choice for your life, only for my own; the position of choice for your own life I hereby give back to you."

"What do you mean?" the other asked, afraid.

"I mean, simply, it's up to you. You decide which way this ends. I will become the counterweight. You do the pulling and bring yourself up. I will even tug a little from here." He began unwinding the rope from around his waist and braced himself anew against the side.

"You cannot mean what you say," the other shrieked. "You would not be so selfish. I am your responsibility. What could be so important that you would let someone die? Do not do this to me."

He waited a moment. There was no change in the tension of the rope.

"I accept your choice," he said, at last, and freed his hands.

Right: Lyonel Feininger, *Rainbow II.*

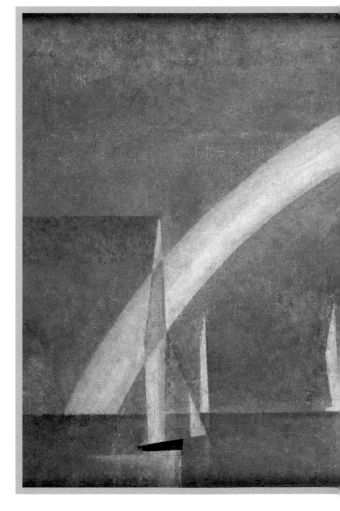

THE MAN WHO DID NOT WISH TO DIE

Allan B. Chinen

L ONG AGO, THERE LIVED A WEALTHY MAN WHO INHERITED A FORTUNE AND LIVED A LIFE OF EASE. He was known as the millionaire. One day, a terrible thought struck him. "I shall die someday! But I want to live forever!" From that moment, he grew troubled in spirit.

Eventually, the millionaire heard tales about the Elixir of Life, possessed by hermits in the mountains. So he left his home, seeking the sages. He climbed the highest peaks and searched all the valleys, but try as he might, he found nobody with the magic elixir. One day, the millionaire met a hunter, and asked the man if he knew of any hermits nearby.

Right: Photograph by Tony Pletts, from the Burning Man Festival 2001. The effigy of the Burning Man himself is traditionally a symbol of death and rebirth, but is seen here as open to individual interpretation. Black Rock City is built especially every year in the Nevada desert to accommodate this Festival.

"No," the hunter replied, "but there is a hand of robbers who live in this forest."

The millionaire felt discouraged. He went to a temple, and prayed to the god of hermits for six days and nights. On the seventh night, the door to the sanctuary flew open. A great light shone from within and the god of hermits stepped out.

"Foolish man!" the god scolded the millionaire. "How do you expect to find the Elixir of Life, when you have lived a life of ease, pleasing only yourself?"

The millionaire trembled, but could not say anything. The god went on. "You know nothing of spiritual discipline, and only those who do can drink the Elixir of Life!"

"But I do not wish to die!" the millionaire pleaded.

The deity paused, took out a small crane made of paper, and gave it to the millionaire. "You lack the wisdom to drink the Elixir of Life, but this crane will take you to the land where no one dies." The god vanished.

In the next moment, the crane grew larger and larger. The millionaire climbed on its back and the bird leaped into the air. They flew for many miles over a great ocean, until they came to a distant shore. The crane landed upon a beach, and the man hastened to the nearest habitation.

"What land is this?" the millionaire asked the first person he met.

"It is the land of perpetual life!" the man replied, and the millionaire rejoiced. The stranger was friendly and helped the millionaire find a home and a job in the town. The millionaire settled down and then noticed how strange his neighbors were. They collected poisonous mushrooms and ate them; they caught venomous snakes and played with them; and they bleached their hair white, so as to look older.

The millionaire asked the people to explain their odd behavior. They said, "We want to die! We are tired of living forever, and we have heard

Archetypes are like riverbeds which dry up when the water deserts them, but which it can find again at any time. An archetype is like an old watercourse along which the water of life has flowed for centuries, digging a deep channel for itself. The longer it has flowed in this channel the more likely it is that sooner or later the water will return to its old bed.

—Carl Gustav Jung

of a place called Paradise, where only the dead can go!"

The millionaire shook his head. "I never want to die!"

The years rolled by and became centuries, and the millionaire became bored with life. Every day was the same as the next. One afternoon, the millionaire walked by the beach. "I hate this life!" he muttered to himself. "If only I could return to my own land and live like an ordinary person, dying in my own time!" Then he had an idea. "If the god of hermits brought me here, perhaps he will let me return home to die." The millionaire said a prayer, and in the next moment something fell from his pocket. It was the old paper crane from the god of hermits, and before his very eyes, the bird grew larger and larger. The millionaire climbed on the crane, and the bird took flight.

As they flew over the sea, a storm struck. The paper wings of the crane crumpled in the rain, and the bird fell into the sea. "Help! Help! I will drown!" the millionaire cried out, floundering in the ocean. The millionaire saw a shark circling. "Help! Help! I don't want to die!" the poor man pleaded with the god of hermits.

In the next instant, the millionaire found himself sprawled on the floor of the mountain temple, screaming for help. The door to the sanctuary opened, a great light filled the hall, and a divine being emerged from the shrine.

"I am a messenger from the god of hermits," the luminous figure said. "He sent you to the land of perpetual life in a dream, because you yearned for immortality. Then you asked for death, so the god sent the storm and the shark to test you. But you only pleaded for your life once more." The messenger looked sadly at the millionaire. "You have no perseverance or faith. Immortality and the secrets of eternity are not for you." The celestial figure then brought out a book. "Go back to your home and family," the shining messenger said, and be content with your lot. The god gives you this book of wisdom. Follow its advice—work hard, raise your children well, provide for their future, and help your neighbors. Then you will fear death no more." With those words, the messenger vanished.

The millionaire returned home with his book of wisdom. And from then on, he followed its counsel. He lived a good, honest life, and when his day finally came, he died with a smile on his lips.

As THE FIREMAN SAID:
Don't book a room over the fifth floor
in any hotel in New York.
They have ladders that will reach further
but no one will climb them.
As the New York Times said:
The elevator always seeks out
the floor of the fire
and automatically opens
and won't shut.
These are the warnings
that you must forget
if you're climbing out of yourself.
If you're going to smash into the sky.

Left: Roger Brown, *Skylab by Minicam.*

RIDING THE ELEVATOR INTO THE SKY

Anne Sexton

Many times I've gone past
the fifth floor,
cranking upward,
but only once
have I gone all the way up,
Sixtieth floor:
small plants and swans bending
into their grave.
Floor two hundred:
mountains with the patience of a cat,
silence wearing its sneakers.
Floor five hundred:
messages and letters centuries old,
birds to drink,
a kitchen of clouds.
Floor six thousand:
the stars,
skeletons on fire,
their arms singing.
And a key,
a very large key,
that opens something—
some useful door—
somewhere—
up there.

THE CLIFF

Charles Baxter

O N THE WAY OUT TO THE CLIFF, THE OLD MAN kept one hand on the wheel. He smoked with the other hand. The inside of the car smelled of wine and cigarette ashes. He coughed constantly. His voice sounded like a version of the cough.

"I used to smoke Camels unfiltered," he told the boy. The dirt road, rutted, dipped hard, and the car bounced. "But I switched brands. Camels interfered with my eating. I couldn't taste what the Duchess cooked up. Meat, salad, Jell-O: it all tasted the same. So I went to low tar. You don't smoke, do you, boy?'

The boy stared at the road and shook his head.

"Not after what I've taught you, I hope not. You got to keep the body pure for the stuff we're doing."

Above: A conflict of spiritual values exists between every generation of Americans, as this telling photograph portrays.   **Right:** This poster conceived by Dr. Timothy Leary, shows him advising people to Turn On, Tune In, and Drop Out. He advocated the use of the hallucinogenic drug, LSD, to experience new spiritual realities, and which would result in the rejection of existing social values. Those believing spiritual experience was harmful to the unprepared saw this as the psychological equivalent of jumping off a cliff.

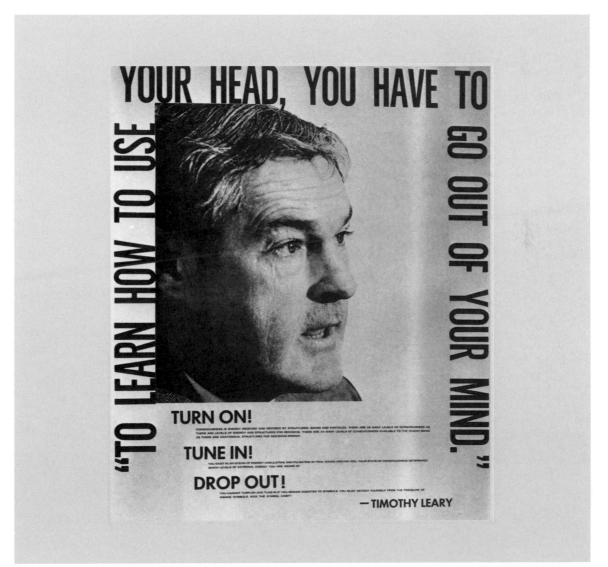

"You don't keep it pure," the boy said.

"I don't have to. It's *been* pure. And, like I say, nobody is ever pure twice."

The California pines seemed brittle and did not sway as they drove past. The boy thought he could hear the crash of the waves in front of them. "Are we almost there?"

"Kind of impatient, aren't you?" the old man said, suppressing his cough. "Look, boy, I told you a hundred times: you got to train your will to do this. You get impatient, and you—"

"—I know, I know. 'You die.' " The boy was wearing a jacket and a New York Mets cap. "I know all that. You taught me. I'm only asking if we're there yet."

"You got a woman, boy?" The old man looked suspicious. "You got a woman?"

"I'm only fifteen," the boy said nervously.

"That's not too old for it, especially around here."

"I've been kissed," the boy said. "Is that the ocean?"

"That's her," the old man said. "Sometimes I think I know everything about you, and then sometimes I don't think I know anything. I hate to take chances like this. You could be hiding something out on me. The magic's no damn good if you're hiding something out on me."

"It'll be good," the boy said, seeing the long line of blue water through the trees. He pulled the visor down lower, so he wouldn't squint. "It'll be real good."

"Faith, hope, charity, and love," the old man recited. "And the spells. Now I admit I have fallen from the path of righteousness at times. But I never forget the spells. You forget them, you die."

"I would not forget them," the boy said.

"You better not be lying to me. You been thieving, sleeping with whores, you been carrying on in the bad way, well, we'll find out soon enough." He stopped the car at a clearing. He turned the key off in the ignition and reached under his seat for a wine bottle. His hands were shaking. The old man unscrewed the cap and took a long swig. He recapped it and breathed out the sweet aroma in the boys direction. "Something for my nerves," he said. "I don't do this every day."

"You don't believe in the spells anymore," the boy said.

"I *am* the spells," the old man shouted. "I invented them. I just hate to see a fresh kid like you crash

Right: Sarah Pletts, *Holy Objects.*

on the rocks on account of *you* don't believe in them."

"Don't worry," the boy said. "Don't worry about me."

They got out of the car together, and the old man reached around into the back seat for his coil of rope.

"I don't need it," the boy said. "I don't need the rope."

"Kid, we do it my way or we don't do it."

The boy took off his shoes. His bare feet stepped over pine needles and stones. He was wearing faded blue jeans and a sweatshirt, with a stain from the old man's wine bottle on it. He had taken off his jacket in the car, but he was still wearing the cap. They walked over a stretch of burnt grass and came to the edge of the cliff.

"Look at those sea gulls down there," the old man pointed. "Must be a hundred." His voice was trembling with nervousness.

"I know about the sea gulls." The boy had to raise his voice to be heard above the surf. "I've seen them."

"You're so smart, huh?" the old man coughed. He drew a cigarette out of his shirt and lit it with his Zippo lighter. "All right, I'm tired of telling you what to do, Mr. Know-It-All. Take off the sweatshirt." The boy took it off. "Now make a circle in the dirt."

"With what?"

"With your foot."

"There isn't any dirt."

"Do like I tell you."

The boy extended his foot and drew a magic circle around himself. It could not be seen, but he knew it was there.

"Now look out at the horizon and tell it what I told you to tell it."

The boy did as he was told.

"Now take this rope, take this end." The old man handed it to him. "God, I don't know sometimes." The old man bent down for another swig of wine. "Is your mind clear?"

"Yeah," the boy said.

"Are you scared?"

"Naw."

"Do you see anybody?"

"Nope."

"You got any last questions?"

"Do I hold my arms out?"

"They do that in the Soviet Union," the old man said, "but they also do it sitting on pigs. That's the kind of people they are. You don't have to hold your arms out. Are you ready? Jump!"

The boy felt the edge of the cliff with his feet, jumped, and felt the magic and the horizon lifting him up and then out over the water, his body parallel to the ground. He took it into his mind to swoop down toward the cliffs, and then to veer away suddenly, and whatever he thought, he did. At first he held on to the rope, but even the old man could see that it was unnecessary, and reeled it in. In his jeans and cap, the boy lifted himself upward, then dove down toward the sea gulls, then just as easily lifted himself up again, rushing over the old man's head before flying out over the water.

He shouted with happiness.

The old man reached down again for his wine.

"The sun!" the old man shouted. "The ocean! The land! That's how to do it!" And he laughed suddenly, his cough all gone. "The sky!" he said at last.

The boy flew in great soaring circles. He tumbled in the air, dove, flipped, and sailed. His eyes were dazzled with the blue also, and like the old man he smelled the sea salt.

But of course he was a teen-ager. He was grateful to the old man for teaching him the spells. But this—the cliffs, the sea, the blue sky, and the sweet wine—this was the old man's style, not his. He loved the old man for sharing the spells. He would think of him always, for that.

But even as he flew, he was getting ideas. It isn't the style of teenagers to fly in broad daylight, on sunny days, even in California. What the boy wanted was something else: to fly low, near the ground, in the cities, speeding in smooth arcs between the buildings, late at night. Very late: at the time the girls are hanging up their clothes and sighing, sighing out their windows to the stagnant air, as the clocks strike midnight. The idea of the pig interested the boy. He grinned far down at the old man, who waved, who had long ago forgotten the dirty purposes of flight.

COSMIC CONSCIOUSNESS
Richard Bucke, 1873

I WAS IN A STATE OF QUIET, ALMOST PASSIVE ENJOYMENT, NOT ACTUALLY THINKING, BUT letting ideas, images, and emotions flow of themselves, as it were, through my mind. All at once, without warning of any kind, I found myself wrapped in a flame-colored cloud. For an instant I thought of fire, an immense conflagration somewhere close by in that great city; the next, I knew that the fire was within myself. Directly afterward there came upon me a sense of exultation, of immense joyousness accompanied or immediately followed by an intellectual illumination impossible to describe. Among other things, I did not merely come to believe, but I saw that the universe is not composed of dead matter, but is, on the contrary, a living Presence; I became conscious in myself of eternal life. It was not a conviction that I would have eternal life, but a consciousness that I possessed eternal life *then*; I saw that all men are immortal; that the cosmic order is such that without any peradventure all things work together for the good of each and all; that the foundation principle of the world, of all the worlds, is what we call love, and that the happiness of each and all is in the long run absolutely certain. The vision lasted a few seconds and was gone; but the memory of it and the sense of the reality of what it taught has remained during the quarter of a century which has since elapsed. I knew that what the vision showed was true... . That view, that conviction, I may say that consciousness, has never, even during periods of the deepest depression, been lost.

Left: Rockwell Kent, *Drifter.* "I was in a state of quiet, almost passive enjoyment, not actually thinking, but letting ideas, images, and emotions flow of themselves, as it were, through my mind."

T E N   M I L E S   W E S T   O F   V E N U S

Judy Troy

A FTER MARVELL LYLE'S HUSBAND, MORGAN, COMMITTED SUICIDE—HIS BODY BEING found on an April evening in the willows that grew along Black Creek—Marvelle stopped going to church. Franklin Sanders, her minister at Venus United Methodist, drove out to her house on a Sunday afternoon in the middle of May to see if he could coax her back. Her house was ten miles west of Venus—seven miles on the highway and three on a two-land road that cut through the open Kansas wheat fields and then wound back through the forest preserve. The woods at this time of year were sprinkled with white blooming pear trees.

Franklin had his radio tuned to Gussie Dell's weekly "Neighbor Talk" program. Gussie was a member of his congregation, and Franklin wanted to see what embarrassing thing she would choose to say today. The week before, she had told a story about her grandson, Norman, drawing a picture of Jesus wearing high heels. "I have respect for Norman's creativity," she had said. "I don't care if Norman puts Jesus in a garter belt."

Today, though, she was on the subject of her sister, whom Franklin had visited in the hospital just the day before. "My sister has cancer," Gussie said. "She may die or she may not. My guess is she won't. I just wanted to say that publicly."

Franklin pulled into Marvell's driveway and turned off the radio too soon to hear whatever Gussie was going to say next; he imagined it was something unfavorable about her sister's husband, who, for years now, had been sitting outside in his chicken shed, watching television. "One of these days I'm going to dynamite him out of

Right: Andrew Lane, *Untitled.*

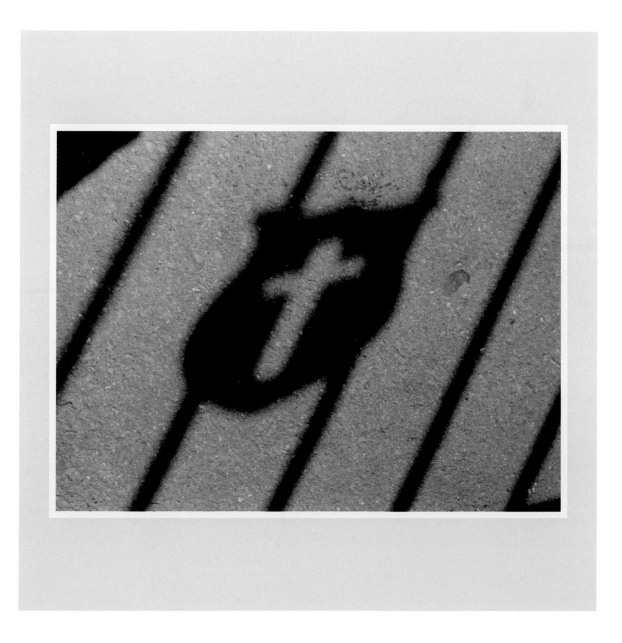

there," Gussie liked to say. She was generally down on marriage, which Franklin couldn't argue with—his own marriage being unhappy, and that fact not a secret among his parishioners.

Franklin parked his new Ford Taurus between Marvelle's old pickup and the ancient Jeep Morgan had driven. Hanging from the Jeep' s rearview mirror were Morgan's military dog tags. He'd been in the Vietnam War, though Franklin had never known any details about it. Morgan Lyle had never been forthcoming about himself, and the few times Franklin had seen him at church Morgan had spent the length of the sermon and most of the service smoking outside. "You have to accept him as he is," Marvelle had once told Franklin. "Otherwise, well, all I'm saying is he doesn't mean anything by what he says and does."

Also in the driveway—just a big gravel clearing, really, between the house and the garage where Morgan had had his motorcycle repair shop—was the dusty van their son, Curtis, drove. He was thirty-one and still living at home. Franklin, who was sixty-three, could remember Curtis as the blond-headed child who had once, in Sunday School, climbed out of a window in order to avoid reciting the Lord's Prayer. Now the grownup Curtis, in faded pants and no shirt, his thinning hair pulled back into a ponytail, opened the door before Franklin had a chance to knock. "Well, come on in, I guess," Curtis said. Behind him Marvelle appeared in the kitchen doorway.

The house was built haphazardly into a hill, and was so shaded with oak and sweetgum trees that the inside—in spring and summer, anyway—was dark during the day. The only light in the room was a small lamp on a desk in the corner, shining down on iridescent feathers and other fly-tying materials. Curtis sat down at the desk and picked up a hook.

"I'll make coffee," Marvelle told Franklin, and he followed her into the kitchen, which was substantially brighter. An overhead light was on, and the walls were painted white. "I thought Sunday afternoons were when you visited the sick," Marvelle said.

"It was, but I do that on Saturdays now. I find other reasons to get out of the house on Sundays." Franklin sat at the kitchen table and watched her make coffee. She was a tall, muscular woman, and she'd lost weight since Morgan's death. Her jeans looked baggy on her; her red hair was longer than it used to be, and uncombed. "You could stand to eat more," Franklin told her.

"You men complain when we're fat and then worry when we're thin."

"When did I ever say you were fat?" Franklin said.

Marvelle turned toward him with the coffeepot in her hand. "You're right. You never did."

Franklin looked down at the table. This afternoon, with his mind on Morgan, and not on himself or his marriage, he'd managed to push aside the memory of an afternoon years ago, when he and Marvelle had found themselves kissing in the church kitchen. "Found themselves" was just how it had seemed to him. It was, like this day, a Sunday afternoon in spring; Marvelle and his wife and two other parishioners had been planting flowers along the front walk. Marvelle had come into the kitchen for coffee just when he had. He wasn't so gray-haired then or so bottom-heavy, and they walked toward each other and kissed passionately, as if they had planned it for months.

"You've always been an attractive woman," he said quietly.

"Don't look so guilty. It was a long time ago." Marvelle sat down across from him as the coffee brewed. "The amazing thing is that it only happened once."

"No," Franklin said, "it's that I allowed it to happen at all."

"Where was God that day? Just not paying attention?" Marvelle asked.

"That was me not paying attention to God," Franklin told her.

Curtis had turned on the radio in the living room, and Franklin could faintly hear a woman singing. Louder was the sound of the coffee brewing. The kitchen table was next to a window that overlooked a sloping wooded hill and a deep ravine. These woods, too, Franklin noticed, had their share of flowering pear trees. "It looks like snow has fallen in a few select places," he said.

"Doesn't it? I saw two deer walking down there his morning. For a moment, I almost forgot about everything else."

Franklin looked at her face, which was suddenly both bright and sad.

"That's interesting," he said carefully, "Because that's what church services do for me."

"Sure they do. Otherwise, you'd lose your place," Marvelle said.

"You don't realize something," Franklin told her. "I'd rather not be the one conducting them. I feel that more and more as I get older. I'd like to sit with the congregation and just partake."

"Would you? Well, I wouldn't. I wouldn't want to do either one." She got up and poured coffee into two mugs and handed one to Franklin. "How do you expect me to feel?" She asked him, standing next to the window. "Do you see God taking a hand in my life? There are people in that congregation who didn't want to see Morgan buried in their cemetery."

"You're talking about two or three people out of a hundred and twenty."

"I bet you felt that way yourself," Marvelle told him.

"You know me better than to think that," Franklin said.

Marvelle sat down and put her coffee on the table in front of her. "All right, I do. Just don't make me apologize."

"When could anybody make you do anything you didn't' t want to do?" Franklin said to her.

Franklin left late in the afternoon, saying goodbye to Curtis after admiring Curtis's fly-tying abilities. Marvelle accompanied him to his car, walking barefoot over the grave. "You'll be walking over coals next," Franklin said, joking.

"Are you trying to sneak God back into the conversation?" Marvelle asked him. She had her hand on his car door as he got in, and she closed the door after him.

"I'm talking about the toughness of your feet," Franklin said through the open window. "I don't expect that much from God. Maybe I used to. But the older I get, the easier I am on him. God's getting older, too, I figure."

"Then put on your seat belt," Marvelle said. She stepped back into a patch of sunlight, so the last thing he saw as he drove away was the sun on her untidy hair and on her pale face and neck.

The woods he passed were gloomier now, with the sun almost level with the tops of the tallest oaks; it was a relief to him to drive out of the trees and into the green wheat fields. The radio was broadcasting a Billy Graham sermon, which Franklin found he couldn't concentrate on. He was wondering about Gussie's sister and if she'd live, and for how long, and what her husband might be thinking out in that chicken shed. When Franklin was at the hospital the day before, Gussie's sister hadn't mentioned her husband. She'd wanted to know exactly how Franklin's wife had redecorated their bedroom.

"Blue curtains and a flowered bedspread," he had told her, and that was all he could remember—nothing about the new chair or the wallpaper or the lamps, all of which he took note of when he went home afterward.

He was also thinking, less intentionally, about Marvelle, who was entering his thoughts as erratically as the crows flying down into the fields he was passing. She was eight or nine years older than when he'd kissed her, but those years had somehow changed into days. When Franklin tried to keep his attention on her grief, it wandered off to her hair, her dark eyes—to every godless place it could. It wasn't until the heard Billy Graham recite, "He maketh me to lie down in green pastures: He leadeth me beside the still water," that Franklin's mind focussed back on Morgan lying in the willows. From that point on he paid attention to the words, falling apart a little when he heard, "Surely goodness and mercy shall follow me all the days of my life," because he didn't know anything more moving, except maybe love, which he didn't feel entitled to; he never had.

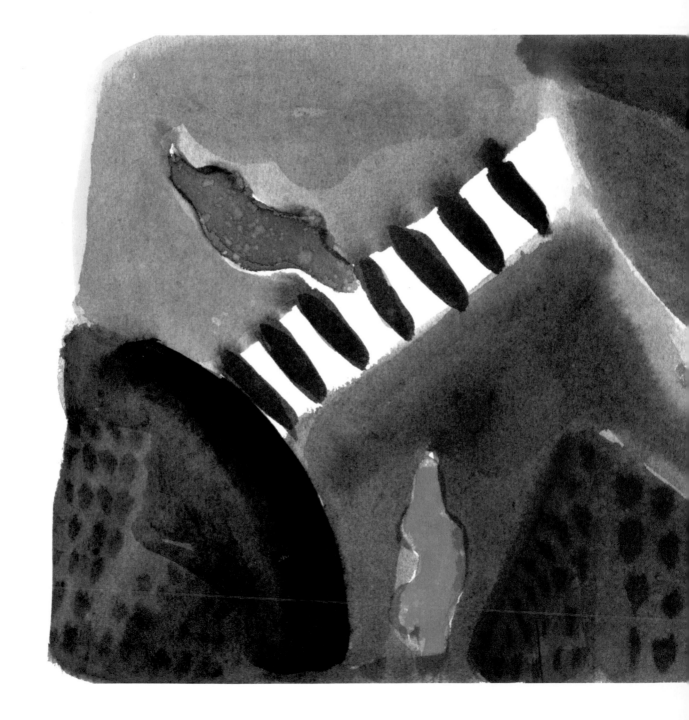

CABDRIVER

Foster Furcolo

I call him Lo because he told me the story of Lo, the poor Indian. It was a typically blustery February Boston morning. Traffic was tied up and drivers were glaring at one another. Everyone was unhappy—everyone, that is, except Lo, my cabdriver.

"You don't seem to be upset that we're not moving," I said.

"Nope," he said, very calmly. He gestured at the lines of traffic in every direction. "We can't go anyplace. What's the use of getting excited?" He lit a cigarette, took a deep puff, and turned around to face me. "You play golf?"

I nodded. "When I can, but I'm not very good."

"Ever get to the tee and find two foursomes along the fairway waiting for a foursome on the green? And another foursome waiting on the next tee?"

Left: John Henshaw, *Crossing—NYC.*

"Lots of times," I said, somewhat mystified as to what he was getting at.

"No place to go," he said. Then he pointed to the surrounding traffic. "Same thing here." He took another drag on the cigarette. "What's the sense of getting excited? Or mad?" He shrugged. "Nothing anyone can do about it. Yet they all get mad and get ulcers."

"I suppose they all have to get someplace," I said, looking at my watch to notify him that I, too, was going to be late for an appointment. "Business meetings or planes or something."

"Oh, sure," he agreed. "That's why they're in cabs. Everybody's got to be someplace except the cabdriver—he's already there. Now look at that guy," he said, pointing to a well-dressed man who had gotten out of his automobile and was talking to a police officer standing helplessly in the midst of the traffic. "That guy is practically having a stroke."

"He's probably late for work."

"I'm never late for work. I'm on time as soon as I get in my cab."

We sat watching the traffic cop trying to untangle the vehicles for a while and then we were on our way.

"You seem to like being a cabdriver," I remarked.

"Wouldn't be anything else," he said.

"Have you tried anything else? " I asked.

He nodded. "Lots of things. I was a yeoman in the navy, then I did office work, and for a while I was a runner for a stockbrokerage firm. But no more of that stuff for me."

"Wouldn't you make more money doing something else?" I asked.

"Oh, sure," he agreed. "If I stayed with that stockbroker I might have even become a millionaire. Who knows? But I've got no ambition."

"Everyone should have ambition," I told him.

"Why?" he asked.

No one had ever asked me that before. Everyone seems to accept the need for ambition the way they accept other self-evident truths.

"Why?" I repeated. "Well, everyone should have ambition or they won't get ahead."

Right: Wallace Berman, *Untitled.*

"So?" he asked.

"So? Well, so they can have a nice home, good clothes, do things for their family. You know, get ahead in life."

"I'm not married and I don't have any family," he told me.

"Even so," I said, "you should still want to get ahead."

And then he said it: "It's just like the Indian," he remarked.

I was nonplussed. "The Indian? What's just like the Indian? What Indian?"

"Lo, the poor Indian," he answered. "I'll tell you the story." He settled back behind the wheel and began. "There was this Indian who was sitting by a river fishing. This white guy used to see him there every day, and whoever he was with, he would point over to the Indian and say to his friend, 'Lo, the poor Indian.' So one day when he was alone, he went over to the Indian and talked to him. 'What are you doing?' he asked. 'Fishing,' the Indian grunted. 'That's all you ever do,' the white guy said. And the Indian just grunted. So the white guy said, 'You ought to get a job and work.' The Indian asked, 'Why?' The white guy said, 'You'll make a lot of money.' The Indian said, 'So?' The white guy said, 'You can invest it and make yourself a lot more money.' What do you think the Indian said to that? He just said, 'So?' Well, the white guy blew his stack. 'So,' he told him, 'If you're rich you can do anything you want to.' The Indian looked at the white man, then turned back to his fishing. 'I'm doing that now,' he said."

The cabdriver laughed. "Lo, the poor Indian." He puffed on his cigarette, then threw it out. "That's me."

I thought about it for a minute. "You're doing what you want?" I said.

"Right."

"And you're satisfied?"

"Right," he said. "Take all that traffic back there. Everybody's

Above: Joseph Stella, *Tree, Cactus, Moon.*

unhappy but me. Why? Because they're not at work; they're not where they're going; they're losing time, or money, or something. But not me. I'm not going anyplace; I'm already there. I'm not losing time, or money, or anything. They got to get out in the cold and walk through snow, or slush, or rain, or whatever. Me, I'm in a nice, warm, dry cab. Do you know when I get out of this cab?"

"No. When do you get out?"

"When I feel like it. When I want coffee or a bite, or I feel like going in someplace and talking to the guys. I get out when I want to, not when I get to someplace where I've got to get out because I've arrived. That *got to* stuff's for the passengers, not for me."

"You've got it made," I said.

"You said it, brother. Now take the good weather," he said. "Summer and spring, or even fall, when the leaves are out and turning. What do you hear people say they want to do on a nice Sunday afternoon? They a want to take a ride, right?"

"A ride through the country," I agreed. "My aunts used to do it every Sunday."

"See the foliage, go by the water, go through the park, ride around someplace," he said. "And not just older people. How about the kids? Do you ever watch the teenagers and the kids in their twenties? What do they want to do except ride around and see the sights?" He pointed toward the Charles. "In the summer you'll see me driving by that river with my windows down. And I'm getting paid for it."

When I got out at my destination, he spoke again. "I don't know what you do for a living, Mister, but whatever it is, I hope you like it. If you don't, I hope you get to be a millionaire so you can do whatever you like. Me, I'm not a millionaire, but I don't have to be one to do whatever I like. I'm doing it now."

As he drove off, I looked after him a long time. Here I was, where I didn't want to be, going into a building to see a man I didn't want to see, and doing some work I didn't want to do.

Lo, the poor cabdriver, I said to myself. And I went about my business.

B A T H I N G   J E S U S
Aliki Barnstone

If he were a word made flesh I would want to wake him from his
godliness
and wash his godliness from him as I bathe his feet in my laughing tears
and dry them with my heat and hair and anoint the topography
of his head with euphoric oil
and comb his beard with electric fingers and pull his face close to mine
to see the multitudes in the pores in his skin, God's intricate
human handiwork in his cheek.
He would see the flame in my eye burning in time's skull, deep
as the first breath that lighted the Milky Way.
I would pull the shirt from his shoulders and the shirt from mine
until our garments lay on the floor, cloth lungs pulsating
with the curtain's white muslin and the little breezes
coming in the window, everything alive,
even the wood floor under our feet warm with the oak's broad
and branching spirit.
And I would pour warm water on his back and thighs and wake
the man in him, wake his hand
reaching for my flushed and water-slicked arm, his palm singeing
the place below my collarbone,
make him taste each word on my tongue, each complex mix of sweet
and bitter and sour and salt
and make him sing out from his body, *the lips, the tongue, the throat,*
the heart, the blood, all the traveling heats of flesh. Praise them.

Right: Minnie Evans, *Drawing #402.*

T H E   R E L U C T A N T   M E S S I A H

Richard Bach

1. There was a Master come unto the earth, born in the holy land of Indiana, raised in the mystical hills east of Fort Wayne.

2. The Master learned of this world in the public schools of Indiana, and as he grew, in his trade as a mechanic of automobiles.

3. But the Master had learnings from other lands and other schools, from other lives that he had lived. He remembered these, and

Right: Cathryn Chase, *Celtic Cave.*

remembering became wise and strong, so that others saw his strength and came to him for counsel.

4. The Master believed that he had power to help himself and all mankind, and as he believed so it was for him, so that others saw his power and came to him to be healed of their troubles, and their many diseases.

5. The Master believed that it is well for any man to think upon himself as a son of God, and as he believed, so it was, and the shops and garages where he worked became crowded and jammed with those who sought his learning and his touch; and the streets outside with those who longed only that the shadow of his passing might fall upon them, and change their lives.

6. It came to pass, because of the crowds, that the several foremen and shop managers bid the Master leave his tools and go his way, for so tightly was he thronged that neither he nor other mechanics had room to work upon the automobiles.

7. So it was that he went into the countryside, and people following began to call him Messiah, and worker of miracles; and as they believed, it was so.

8. If a storm passed as he spoke, not a raindrop touched a listener's head; the last of the multitude heard his words as clearly as the first, no matter lightning nor thunder in the sky about. And always he spoke to them in parables.

9. And he said unto them, "Within each of us lies the power of our consent

Preparation for the spiritual journey usually begins with self-examination. Reflecting on personal history and letting go of resentments and regrets releases us from the past.

—Frances Vaughan

to health and to sickness, to riches and to poverty, to freedom and to slavery. It is we who control these, and not another."

10. A mill-man spoke and said, "Easy words for you, Master, for you are guided as we are not, and need not toil as we toil. A man has to work for his living in this world."

11. The Master answered and said, "Once there lived a village of creatures along the bottom of a great crystal river.

12. "The current of the river swept silently over them all—young and old, rich and poor, good and evil, the current going its own way, knowing only its own crystal self.

13. "Each creature in its own manner clung tightly to the twigs and rocks of the river bottom, for clinging was their way of life, and resisting the current what each had learned from birth.

14. "But one creature said at last, 'I am tired of clinging. Though I cannot see it with my eyes, I trust that the current knows where it is going. I shall let go, and let it take me where it will. Clinging, I shall die of boredom.'

15. "The other creatures laughed and said, 'Fool! Let go, and that current you worship will throw you tumbled and smashed across the rocks, and you will die quicker than boredom!'

16. "But the one heeded them not, and taking a breath did let go, and at once was tumbled and smashed by the current across the rocks.

17. "Yet in time, as the creature refused to cling again, the current lifted him free from the bottom, and he was bruised and hurt no more.

18. "And the creatures downstream, to whom he was a stranger, cried, 'See a miracle! A creature like ourselves, yet he flies! See the Messiah, come to save us all!'

19. "And the one carried in the current said, 'I am no more Messiah than you. The river delights to lift us free, if only we dare let go. Our true work is this voyage, this adventure.'

20. "But they cried the more, 'Savior!' all the while clinging to the rocks, and when they looked again he was gone, and thy were left alone making legends of a Savior."

21. And it came to pass when he saw that the multitude thronged him the more day on day, tighter and closer and fiercer than ever they had, when he saw that they pressed him to heal them without rest, and feed them always with his miracles, to learn for them and to live their lives, he went alone that day unto a hilltop apart, and there he prayed.

22. And he said in his heart, Infinite Radiant Is, if it be thy will, let this cup pass from me, let me lay aside this impossible task. I cannot live the life of one other soul, yet ten thousand cry to me for life. I'm sorry I allowed it all to happen. If it be thy will, let me go back to my engines and my tools and let me live as other men.

23. And a voice spoke to him on the hilltop, a voice neither male nor female, loud nor soft, a voice infinitely kind. And the voice said unto him, "Not my will, but thine be done. For what is thy will is mine for thee. Go thy way as other men, and be thou happy on the earth."

24. And hearing, the Master was glad, and gave thanks and came down from the hilltop humming a little mechanic's song. And when the throng pressed him with its woes, beseeching him to heal for it and learn for it and feed it nonstop from his understanding and to entertain it with his wonders, he smiled upon the multitude and said pleasantly unto them, "I quit."

25. For a moment the multitude was stricken dumb with astonishment.

26. And he said unto them, "If a man told God that he wanted most of all to help the suffering world, no matter the price to himself, and God answered and told him what he must do, should the man do as he is told?"

27. "Of course, Master!" cried the many. "It should be pleasure for him to suffer the tortures of hell itself, should God ask it!"

28. "No matter what those tortures, nor how difficult the task?"

29. "Honor to be hanged, glory to be nailed to a tree and burned, if so be that God has asked," said they.

30. "And what would you do," the Master said unto the multitude, "if God spoke directly to your face and said, 'I COMMAND THAT YOU BE HAPPY IN THE WORLD, AS LONG AS YOU LIVE.' What would you do then?"

31. And the multitude was silent, not a voice, not a sound was herd upon the hillsides, across the valleys where they stood.

32. And the Master said unto the silence, "In the path of our happiness shall we find the learning for which we have chosen this lifetime. So it is that I have learned this day, and choose to leave you now to walk your own path, as you please."

33. And he went his way through the crowds and left them, and he returned to the everyday world of men and machine.

A C K N O W L E D G M E N T S

First and foremost, we would like to thank Jeremy Tarcher for his vision in creating this anthology series, and for his dedication and unwavering support in guiding the book towards completion. Our greatest appreciation is also extended to Robert Bly, Jean Houston, Robert A. Johnson, and Andrew Weil for their essential contributions to this series. To John Beebe, editor of the *San Francisco Institute Library* Journal, Alan B. Chinen, Connie Zweig, and the many members of the Jungian, transpersonal, and holistic medicine communities for their insights and suggestions concerning the selection of materials for these books—our deepest thanks. The talents of several people came together to make this unique collection of stories and art into the beautiful volume you hold in your hands. Mark Robert Waldman whose skills as an author and editor shine in the choices he made for the book carefully selected the texts. Julie Foakes, whose talents as an art researcher can never be praised enough, chose all the images. Marion Kocot brought order and harmony to the words with her talented editing skills. Sara Carder at Tarcher Putnam provided constant encouragement and handholding throughout the process. Joel Fontinos, the publisher at Tarcher Putnam, guided us with enthusiasm and praise. And Kristen Garneau brought text and images together in the elegant layout of the pages. To you all A HUGE THANK YOU!

—Philip and Manuela Dunn of The Book Laboratory Inc.

ABOUT THE EDITOR

Mark Robert Waldman is a therapist and the author and editor of numerous books, including *The Spirit of Writing, Love Games, Dreamscaping* and *The Art of Staying Together.* He was founding editor of Transpersonal Review, covering the fields of transpersonal and Jungian psychology, religious studies, and mind/body medicine.

ABOUT THE BOOK CREATORS

Philip Dunn and Manuela Dunn Mascetti have created many best-selling volumes, including *The Illustrated Rumi*, Huston Smith's *Illustrated World's Religions*, Stephen Hawking's *The Illustrated A Brief History of Time* and *The Universe in a Nutshell*, and Thomas Moore's *The Illustrated Care of the Soul.* They are the authors of *The Illustrated Rumi, The Buddha Box*, and many other books.

ABOUT THE INTRODUCTORY AUTHOR

Jean Houston, Ph.D., is the best-selling author of many books, including *Jump Time, The Possible Human, The Search for the Beloved*, and *A Mythic Life.* She is co-director of the Foundation for Mind Research and is a consultant to UNICEF and other international agencies. Past President of the Association for Humanistic Psychology, she has received numerous awards, including Teacher/Educator of the Year and the INTA Humanitarian of the Year.

T E X T   A C K N O W L E D G M E N T S

Every effort has been made to trace all copyright holders of the material included in this volume, whether companies or individuals. Any omission is unintentional and we will be pleased to correct any errors in future editions of this book.

Grateful acknowledgment is made to Aliki Barnstone for permission to reproduce the story *Bathing Jesus,* also published in *Wild With It* by Sheep Meadow Press, 2001, in *Voices of Light: Spiritual and Visionary Poems by Women Around the World* by Shambhala Publications, 1999, and in *The Drunken Boat,* © 2000 by Aliki Barnstone.

The Bridge from *Friedman's Fables* by Edwin Friedman, © 1990 by The Guilford Press, is reproduced here by kind permission of the publisher.

Brother Jake and the Preacher from *Just Plain Folks* by Lorraine Johnson-Coleman, © 1998 by Lorraine Johnson-Coleman, is reprinted here by kind permission of Little, Brown, and Company, Inc.

Catholic Dreams from *Dreams Are Wiser Than Men* by Richard Russo, © 1987 by North Atlantic Books, Berkeley, California, is reprinted here kind permission of the publisher.

A City of Churches, ©1972 by Donald Barthelme, is reprinted here by kind permission of The Wylie Agency, Inc.

The Cliff from *Harmony of the World* by Charles Baxter and published by University of Missouri Press, © 1984 by the Curators of the University of Missouri, is reprinted here by kind permission of publisher and author.

Forever Young, ©1988 by Ronald Steel, has been reprinted here by kind permission of the author.

From Skinhead to Godhead © 1999 by Dan Millman, has been reprinted by kind permission of the Candice Fuhrman Literary Agency.

Homeless, © 2000 by Doris Colmes, has been reprinted by kind permission of the author.

I Don't Write to God No More, a letter from *The Color Purple,* © 1982 by Alice Walker, has been reprinted by kind permission of Harcourt, Inc.

Grateful acknowledgment is made to Lhakdor for His Holiness the Dalai Lama, for kind permission to reprint *Making Your Life Meaningful,* © 2000 by the Dalai Lama.

Grateful acknowledgment is made to Allan B. Chinen for permission to reprint *The Man Who Did Not Wish to Die* from *Once Upon a Midlife,* © 1992 by Allan B. Chinen.

Meeting Helen Keller from *Public Like a Frog* by Jean Houston, © 1993 by Quest Books. Reproduced by kind permission of Quest Books and Jean Houston.

Mystery from *Kitchen Table Wisdom* by Rachel Naomi Remen, M.D., © 1996 by Rachel Naomi Remen, has been reprinted by kind permission of Riverhead Books, a division of Penguin Putnam, Inc.

The Reluctant Messiah from *Illusions: The Adventures of a Reluctant Messiah* by Richard Bach, © 1977 by Richard Bach. Reprinted by kind permission of Dell Publishing, a division of Random House, Inc.

Riding the Elevator Into the Sky from *The Awful Rowing Toward God* by Anne Sexton, first published in The New Yorker, © 1975 by Loring Conant, Jr., executor of the Estate of Anne Sexton, has been reprinted by kind permission of Houghton Mifflin Company. All rights reserved.

Siddhartha from *Siddhartha* by Herman Hesse, © 1951 by New Directions Publishing Corp., has been reprinted by kind permission of New Directions Publishing Corporation and Laurence Pollinger Limited.

Ten Miles West of Venus, © 1997 by Judy Troy, reprinted by kind permission of Georges Borchardt, Inc.

ART ACKNOWLEDGMENTS

Page 17   Grant Wood, *Parson Weems' Fable,* 1939, oil on canvas, 1970.43; Amon Carter Museum, Fort Worth, Texas

Page 18   Nick Andrew, *Davidea*

Page 20   Dilip Mehta/Contact Press Images

Page 22   Sarah Pletts, *Buddhist Shrine,* 1993, Photomontage, 12" x 18"

Page 26   Cathryn Chase, *Gateway to Other Worlds*

Page 29   Warner Bros. Courtesy of Ronald Grant Archive

Page 32   Courtesy of The Advertising Archives

Page 33   Lyonel Feininger, *Church of Heiligenhafen;* Reynolda House, Museum of American Art, Winston-Salem, North Carolina; © 2002 Artists Rights Society (ARS), New York / VG Bild-Kunst, Bonn

Page 38 detail
& page 39   Robert Gwathmey, *Belle;* Reynolda House, Museum of American Art, Winston-Salem, North Carolina; © Estate of Robert Gwathmey/Licensed by VAGA, New York, NY

Page 40   Jack Levine, *The Visit from the Second World;* Reynolda House, Museum of American Art, Winston-Salem, North Carolina; Jack Levine/Licensed by VAGA, New York, NY

Page 44   James Van Der Zee, American, 1886-1983, *Daddy Grace at the Altar with Choir,* 1938, vintage gelatin silver print, 19.3 x 24.5 cm, The Sandor Family Collection in honor of The School of the Art Institute of Chicago, 1994.898, photo reproduction © The Art Institute of Chicago. All Rights Reserved. Copyright © Donna Van Der Zee

Page 49 | Marsden Hartley, *American Indian Symbols,* 1914, oil on canvas, 1984.16; Amon Carter Museum, Fort Worth, Texas

Page 54 | Georgia O'Keeffe, American, 1887-1986. *Black Cross, New Mexico,* 1929, oil on canvas, 99.2 x 76.3 cm. Art Institute Purchase Fund, 1943.95, photo reproduction © The Art Institute of Chicago. All Rights Reserved

Page 57 | Audrey Flack, *Bounty;* Reynolda House, Museum of American Art, Winston-Salem, North Carolina. Courtesy of the artist and Louis K. Meisel Gallery, New York

Page 65 | Morton Livingstone Schamberg, *Figure,* 1913, oil on canvas, 1984.16; Amon Carter Museum, Fort Worth, Texas

Page 67 | Cathryn Chase, *Sunken Temple*

Page 68 | Florine Stettheimer, American, 1871-1944, *Portrait of Virgil Thomson,* 1930, oil on canvas, 97.2 x 51.1 cm, Gift of Virgil Thomson, 1975.677, photo reproduction © The Art Institute of Chicago. All Rights Reserved

Page 71 | Getty Images/Hulton Archive

Page 72 | Julie Foakes

Page 78 | Sarah Pletts, *Target,* 1996, oil on paper, 838 x 1143 mm

Page 81 | Getty Images/Hulton Archive

Page 84 | Paul Steel/The Stock Market

Page 86 | Sarah Pletts, *Glitter Buddha,* 1994, digital image

Page 87 | National Space Science Data Center

Page 90 | The Apollo Mission Principal Investigator, Dr. Richard J. Allenby, Jr. and National Space Science Data Center

Page 93   Getty Images/Hulton Archive

Page 97   David F. Barry, *Sitting Bull or Tata'nka l'Yota'nka,* ca. 1886, collodion chloride print, P1967.466, Amon Carter Museum, Fort Worth, Texas

Page 98   Andrew Lane

Page 102   Alfred Stieglitz, American 1864-1946, *Georgia O'Keeffe,* 1920, solarized palladium print, 25. X 20.2 cm, The Alfred Stieglitz Collection, 1949.745, photo reproduction © The Art Institute of Chicago. All Rights Reserved

Page 103 top   Barry Peterson, *Hands, variation 2,* compressed charcoal on newsprint, 12" x 12"

Page 103 btm   Barry Peterson, *Hands, variation 3,* compressed charcoal on newsprint, 12" x 12"

Page 106 detail &
page 107   Sarah Pletts, *Peace Shrine,* 1994, Mixed Media

Page 111   Lyonel Feininger, *Rainbow II;* Reynolda House, Museum of American Art, Winston-Salem, North Carolina; © 2002 Artists Rights Society (ARS), New York / VG Bild-Kunst, Bonn

Page 113   Burning Man 2001, Photography by Tony Pletts

Page 116   Roger Brown, *Skylab by Minicam;* Reynolda House, Museum of American Art, Winston-Salem, North Carolina

Page 119   Getty Images/Hulton Archive

Page 121   Sarah Pletts, *Holy Objects,* 1993, Photomontage, 12" x 18"

Page 124   Rockwell Kent, *Drifter,* 1933, wood engraving, 1997.90; Amon Carter Museum, Fort Worth, Texas

Page 127   Andrew Lane

Page 130   Julie Foakes

Page 132   John Henshaw, Crossing-NYC

Page 135   Wallace Berman, *Untitled,* 1959, from the series Portraits of Jay DeFeo. Gelatin silver print, Sight 5 x 4 7/8 in. (12.7 x 12.38 cm.), Whitney Museum of American Art, New York; gift of the Lannan Foundation, 96.243.9

Page 136   Joseph Stella, *Tree, Cactus, Moon;* Reynolda House, Museum of American Art, Winston-Salem, North Carolina

Page 139   Minnie Evans, American, 1892-1987, *Drawing #402,* 1967, acrylic with gold metallic paint, touches of oil paint, and black pen and red colored pencil on off-white wove card, 28 x 35 cm, Robert A. Lewis Fund Gift, 1982.119, photo reproduction © The Art Institute of Chicago. All Rights Reserved. Courtesy of Luise Ross Gallery, New York

Page 141   Cathryn Chase, *Celtic Cave*

Cover   Frederic Remington, *A Figure of the Night,* 1908, oil on canvas. Courtesy Sid Richardson Collection of Western Art, Fort Worth, Texas